# MODI'S MIRACLE
# SHIFT *to* RIGHT

# MODI's MIRACLE SHIFT *to* RIGHT

**N Vittal,** IAS (Retd)
Former Central Vigilance Commissioner (CVC)
Government of India

Manas Publications
(We Convert Fighters into Writers)
New Delhi - 110 002 (INDIA)

**MANAS PUBLICATIONS**
**(We Convert Fighters into Writers)**
(Publishers, Library Suppliers, Importers & Exporters)
4402/5-A, Ansari Road (Opp. HDFC Bank)
Darya Ganj, New Delhi - 110 002 (India)
**Phones : Off.: 011-23260783, 23265523, Res.: 011-23842660**
**E-mail : manaspublications@gmail.com**
**manaspublications@yahoo.com**
**Website : www.manaspublications.in**



**ISBN 978-81-7049-528-4**
**₹ 795.00**



*Designed at*
**Manas Publications**

*Printed in India at*
R.K. Printers, Delhi
and published by Mrs Suman Lata for
Manas Publications, 4402/5-A,
Ansari Road (Opp HDFC Bank),
Darya Ganj, New Delhi - 110002 (INDIA)

# Preface

Narendra Modi leading the Bharatiya Janata Party (BJP) and its allies as the National Democratic Alliance (NDA) blazed a new chapter in the political history of India when he won a shining victory in the Lok Sabha elections of 2014. This was indeed a watershed in the political history of independent India. It marked a decisive shift to the Right in Indian politics.

The election results of 2014 are indeed very important in their long-term impact on the evolution of India as a modern democratic nation which is well-governed and fulfil its destiny as a great nation in all senses – social, economic, political in the comity of nations. As I see it, this is a great opportunity in the evolution and emergence of India as a nation which has its own culture and unique spiritual identity. The Left of centre ideology that prevailed in the governance of our country was conspicuously cut off from any remote identification with our history, culture and religion of India and anything that can be remotely called Hindu. In fact, the expression 'Hinduism' itself was shunned. It was identified as an expression denoting a communal and backward looking mindset. The brave new exiting exercise in which the Modi government has landed itself is an exciting one of articulating and putting in place a new political right in India based on our own Sanatana Dharma. This is the source of our culture and soul of our motherland Bharatmata.

The most important meaning of 2014 election is that the people of our country after 70 years of experimenting with the left of centre have decided that we must try the politics of the right of centre for the next phase of our governance from 2014 to 2019. The historic victory of BJP in 2017 Assembly elections in four States – Uttar Pradesh, Uttarakhand, Goa and Manipur – has tremendously increased the faith of people in the Right governance of Modi government. Recently BJP won all the three municipal corporations in Delhi for the third term in a row, handing a humiliating defeat to the Aam Aadmi Party and the Congress. These election results carry wider national ramifications and the BJP will only add to its image to invincibility and leave a divided opposition further demoralised in the run up to the national elections in 2019.

The new Indian political right shaped by the Modi government is thanks to the combined efforts of Narendra Modi and Mohan Bhagwat, Sarsanghchalak of RSS is a very positive and welcome development. Based on the Sanatana Dharma which is the soul of our culture, it is open minded and ideally suited for good governance.

In this book, I have tried to articulate how this change is taking place and how the relentless attack on the Modi government by the establishment 'secular' intelligentsia is only exposing its own weakness and inadequacies that have gone unchallenged during the last seven decades.

## ❖ *Preface* ❖

As a member of the IAS belonging to the Gujarat cadre (1960 batch), I spent 42 years of my life in public governance. I had worked closely with top leaders in policy making levels both in the State of Gujarat and in the Government of India (GoI) for more than four decades of independent India. I, therefore have an insider's perspective based on actual experience, in understanding the dynamics of how this tectonic shift to the Right in the governing philosophy of the GoI took place, its significance and other dimensions.

This book reflects my perceptions of this shift and describes how Modi's political philosophy differs from the Nehruvian one which prevailed so far and whether his programmes have a reasonable chance of the success.

N Vittal

# Contents

# 1

# My Roots

Before proceeding further, at this stage I must make a full and fair disclosure. This is about my background and bias.

I am immensely proud of my motherland, the great Bharatavarsha. I am one of the billions of the children of Bharatmata.

I am very proud of her great traditions, art and culture, apart from her unique spiritual framework Sanatana Dharma.

In one word, I am an unabashed believer in the Right of Indian politics. Why?

I was brought up in a traditional Hindu Madhwa Deshastha middle class family. Right from my childhood I have imbibed those values. My father and mother were both religious. They believed very strongly in the need for maintaining one's intellectual, moral and financial integrity.

They also strongly believed that if you are straight forward and have faith in God, God will help you and take care of your needs. I have seen my father a legal practitioner on the criminal side serving as Assistant Public Prosecutor, live on the principle of total faith in Lord Venkateswara or Narayana. He was also particularly devoted to Devi Akilandeswari of Thiruvanaikovil (Tiruchirappalli in Tamil Nadu). Cycling to the temple every Friday evening was ritual with him.

My mother tongue is Marathi. That fact gave me certain special advantages.

I belong to the Maharashtrian Deshastha Brahmin community who migrated in the last quarter of 17th century from Maharashtra to Thanjavur in Tamil Nadu. They were closely linked with the governance of the Maharashtrian rulers. The Deshastha Brahmins as a community were perceived as those who were bright and competent. Above all they were also considered to be honest by and large. They were naturally preferred as advisers and good for governance. The British government used to select and post people from this community as cashiers in most of the offices, especially the railways.

The Maharashtrian rulers tempted them with incentives of land grants to migrate along with them to the south and establish their rule in Thanjavur.

The Maharashtrian rulers replaced the rule of Nayaks in Thanjavur. The Nayaks traced their powers claiming the legacy of the Vijayanagara Empire going back 500 years to the period of Krishna Devaraya in the 16th century. He was the most glorious king of the Vijayanagara Empire established in the 14th century under the inspiration of their Guru Vidyaranya, by the Yadava rulers Harihara and Bhukka of Devagiri.

It was possibly the first empire in Indian history in recent times which was specially committed to Hinduism, more specifically to the concept and way of life under the Sanatana

Dharma. This was needed as the Mughal rule in the north was spreading south of Vindhyas.

Sanatana Dharma, in turn has a very long tradition in our country. It is known from Vedic times. Vedas are believed to be at least 3,000 to 5,000 years old. In Vedic times our country India was called as Bharatavarsha or Bharata Khanda.

# 2

# Sanatana Dharma and Its Evolution

The Vedas which are the basis of our Sanatana Dharma or Hinduism are rooted in a global vision. This philosophy treats the entire world as one family. The concept of *vasudhaiva kutumbakam* (the world is one family) is a fundamental aspect of faith in this spiritual framework.

How did this global vision evolve?

For understanding this we have to go beyond history in to proto-history. In fact, we must go back in times by millions of years.

The breaking of the genetic code and the mind boggling advances in bioengineering and genetic engineering along with digital technology has thrown up totally unexpected insights regarding Sanatana Dharma.

With the help of modern genetics and advances in computer and digital technology, we can trace the migration of human race from the time it originally evolved on our earth. The human race is believed to have originated millions of years ago in Africa at the macro level from mammals. It spread to other continents of earth. Even at the level of the individual, thanks to the breaking of the genetic code, today any person can at a very reasonable cost of a few dollars trace his/her complete genetic genealogy!

Gurnek Bains who is apparently an Indian Sikh married to an Australian woman and living in Canada has come with an interesting book recently (2015), called *Cultural DNA: The Psychology of Globalization*. He gives a very fresh and exciting interpretation about why while violence has been the hallmark of evolution of human race or life itself under the Darwinian principle of survival of fittest, concepts like *vasudhaiva kutumbakam* or *ahimsa* (non-violence) could have evolved?

It is here Gurnek Bains comes with an interesting information and perspective.

Thanks to the blockbuster film 'Jurassic Park', every child is aware of the fact that 65 million years ago, life on earth was dominated by gargantuan animals like the dinosaurs. How did they disappear and make way for smaller animals like humans and other animals we see today to evolve?

65 million years ago there was a freak strike of a huge asteroid in the Gulf of Mexico near the Caribbean. This disaster caused extensive damage to all major forms of life. For millions of years the earth was covered by a dark cloud which blocked even the sunlight.

While the dinosaurs could not survive, human beings and similar small smart forms of life were flexible enough to adapt to the drastically changed environmental conditions and managed to survive and thrive. Ultimately, they went on to evolve into Homo sapiens and other forms of flora and fauna, we see today. In most of the places, there were forests and wild animals. So killing animals and violence was the only way by which the human race could have survived.

The narrative so far is familiar. All of us know that Darwin's theory of survival of the fittest provides a credible explanation of the ingrained human nature for violence and selfishness. But this does not explain all types of human behaviour.

For example, in times of natural disasters like flood or earthquakes, many humans display divine qualities of utter selflessness and go to great extent to help save as may be possible. How to justify this?

The December 2015 rains of Chennai resulted in the floods for a week thanks to a century old record of rain. This disaster provided ample examples of the good and bad side of human beings. There were cases of sheer greed and selfishness. There were also many noble deeds of people scarifying their own life to save others.

Without sacrificing the selfishness principle, one can still explain this anomaly, by sublimating self-interest to collective interest or enlightened self-interest.

Karl von Frisch, an Austrian ethologist who won the Noble Prize for his study of the dance of the honey bees and their characters came up with the explanation of 'territorial imperative'. This explains how each creature dominates its own place and is reluctant to admit others inside it.

If selfishness was dominant in the context of Darwin's survival of the fittest, altruism can be explained only on the principle of the survival of life by sublimation of selfishness as enlightened self-interest.

Ethology brought out the similarity between human and animals in behaviour. Territorial imperative became a code word to describe the selfishness of every animal for its own space. In the Darwinian view selfishness is the dominating aspect.

When it comes to altruism, Gurnek Bains in his book offers literally an out of the world explanation and narrative!

He highlights an interesting piece of information from astronomy and palaeontology.

Apart from the periodic attacks by asteroids there were strikes by meteors also. The most serious meteor strike in fairly recent times was the 1908 Tunguska event in Siberia. The meteor strike were led to great disaster, but on a much smaller scale compared to major events in the past. Nevertheless, massive devastation was caused to a very large area affecting the flora and fauna.

In addition to meteors and asteroids, there were simultaneously very wide ranges of volcanic activity during the period of millions after the Jurassic disaster, which killed the dinosaurs.

75,000 years ago there was much violent volcanic activity. But they had different effect from the meteor/asteroid effects. The impact of this activity was that all the trees were destroyed and the whole forest area became a vast savanna or pampas or plain and level grassland. In these areas, which include bulk of Asia, Australia and the Far East, the life forms that survived were the human race, animals like cows, dogs and horses. There were of course, wild breeds like the lions and tigers in the forests but in the environment of vast level grass lands which were level that evolved there was no alternative for the human race to survive but to invent agriculture and hold on to dear life.

In the changed environment, the human beings started realising the need for keeping the dog as a friend and especially for protection and keep watch over their cattle grazing activities. The cow became very significant because that was the main source of nutrition. Our worshipping of the *gomatha* or the concept of *Kamadhenu* etc can be traced to this combination of geological activities and the changes in the life forces that survived the human imperative to somehow survive. Therefore, the religions that originated in the Indian subcontinent which are called Indic regions like Hinduism, Jainism, Sikhism and Buddhism highlight and emphasised the need for love of animals. This lies on the root of the concept of *ahimsa*.

This approach naturally led to the Upanishad's dictum of *sarve bhavantu sukhinah, sarve santu niramayah, sarve bhadrani pashyantu, ma kashchid duhkha-bhag-bhavet*. This was famously quoted by Arun Jaitley as Finance Minister in his first NDA budget of 2014. In short, this articulates the soul of the political right in India. The left did not have this all inclusive macro view. In fact, it accuses the right of being exclusive or elitist.

This distinct difference from the western thought based on Darwinism and the central role played by selfishness and violence comes out sharp when we realise that our Indic religions hold love and non-violence as central and important aspect by which the right traces its root to the cultural ethos of our country.

# 3

# Unique Features of Sanatana Dharma

There are many other differences. For example, in Sanatana Dharma, the mother is worshipped as a God. In fact, she gets the prime importance. The Upanishadic invocations call for *matrudevo bhava, pitrudevo bhava, acharyadevo bhava, atithidevo bhava*. The idea of treating mother as Goddess or looking at women as mother is distinctly different from the western approach. In fact, it was this respect for women which Vivekananda articulated in his famous Chicago address and his visit in 1893 to United States that drew attention. On the other hand, in the west, if a woman is addressed as mother, she is likely to take it as an indication of her age and appearance. Hence she may not welcome it. This respect for women is totally alien to western concept. When it comes to politics, the attitude of the Right represented by the BJP and its allies is labelled by the secular intelligentsia as being conservative and backward looking against the modern concept of gender equality. For these sentry people, it is 'father India' and not 'mother India'.

In the 1970s, the Lebanese thinker Edward Said's book *Orientalism*, had a great impact in the intellectual circles because of a serious correction in perspective it brought to the studies on the eastern philosophy by western serenity from the easterners point of view and thought and religion on western thinkers were championing the colonial rule as a method of civilising the colonial region.

The word orientalism itself Said points out was an expression coined by western thinkers particularly the French who followed Napoleon in to Egypt.

It is said that Napoleon addressed his soldiers in front of the pyramids, "three thousand years of history are gazing on you!" The conquering Westerners who colonised the East felt that they were carrying a great mission. They were carrying out the 'White man's burden' of colonising nations.

The explosive growth of colonialism and imperialism in the 19th century followed the industrial revolution of the 18th century which was launched in Britain. Leading colonial powers like Britain and France were acutely aware of the impact of exploitation of natural resources of the colonies. It was the white man's burden. This provided a raison d'être for their exploitation of colonialism as a source of raw material and markets.

Western scholars studying eastern philosophies had tried to interpret this from their perspective. Similarly, the only mission of the Christian missionaries was to spread the word of the Lord. Their activities came in as an additional rationale for imperialism and colonialism.

The imperialists and colonisers were badly in need of a new narrative to justify morally their brazen exploitation of human and physical resources of the poor colonies. The so-called White man's burden of a civilising mission was the handy tool to camouflage crude economic self-interest with a plausible moral veneer.

The Christian missionaries with their Holy mission to spread the Word of our Lord provided the religious justification for Imperialism. Intellectual heft to justify colonialism and imperialism was provided by the so-called oriental experts and scholars like Max Mueller and TE Lawrence of Arabia.

Fortunately, even though the original intentions behind the oriental studies were different, in the long run, the contributions of the scholars proved to be a great gain for humanity as a whole. Scholars like Max Mueller brought the glories of Sanskrit particularly Kalidasa and the *Bhagawad Gita* to the knowledge of western people.

Similarly, French scholars developed the concept of orientalism and brought the Indian contribution to areas of knowledge of mathematics, algebra, trigonometry, number theory, Ayurveda, astronomy, architecture, dance and music. There was a time, when many Indians thought in my father's generation India, felt really proud that a German like Max Mueller appreciated our wealth cf knowledge and beauty of Sanskrit as brought out in the biography of Max Mueller *Scholar Extraordinary: The Life of Professor the Rt. Hon. Friedrich Max Muller* by Nirad C Chaudhuri. His name was even Sanskritised as Mokshamoola and in the Tiruvallikeni Parthasarathy Temple, *archanas* were performed for his health and recovery when he was in his last days. The pride of the earlier 20th century citizens of the country like India and the Arab countries in the corporal sprits in the culture was an unexpected consequence of the Western scholars' effect at bringing a convincing narrative for justifying their colonialism. The concept of White man's burden which the British introduced in India can be easily understood in the context of what Edward Said has brought out in his book *Orientalism*. It is now easy to understand how those Indians like Mahatma Gandhi, Jawaharlal Nehru and veterans of the 20th century freedom struggle looked at India from different perspective than those Indians who were not exposed to this earlier. For example, Aurobindo Ghosh's father was an Anglophile and initially Aurobindo had an English name (Audrey). This is mentioned in the book *Father India* by Konraed Ecch I referred to above. Smriti Irani's simple explanation in 2014 after BJP's victory when Modi became PM was Father India has been replaced by Mother India. It brings out clarity and precisely of the tectonic change symbolised by the rise of the Indian political Right and Narendra Modi.

The book *Father India* labels those who believe in the traditional concept of Sanatana Dharma look upon India as their mother (Mother India) keeping in tune with the Upanishadic invocation *mathru devo bhava.*

Those who first learned about our country in depth through English or other European writers are labelled as those for whom our country is Father India.

How can we classify the great spirit of reform and regeneration of the second half of the 19th century especially in beginning and the first three decades of the twentieth century in the rest of India?

As I see it a great majority were the Children of Father India. Nevertheless there were a powerful set of leaders like Pandit Madan Mohan Malavia, Netaji Subhas Chandra Bose,

Sardar Vallabhbhai Patel, Swami Vivekananda, Syama Prasad Mukherjee, Sri Aurobindo were children of mother India.

All of us watched the emotional high point of Narendra Modi's first visit to the parliament after his electoral triumph in the General Elections of April 2014.

That moment signalled to the entire world the tectonic shift of India to the political Right.

Mother India had for the first time asserted herself as the governing creed of Government of India.

I want to make one point clear. The label Father India and Mother India are used here as a handy label to classify the source of inspiration so far as a particular leader is concerned. I am not at all suggesting that Mother India patriots are better than Father India patriots. It is not meant as disrespect for any of them. NOT even a single one.

What they indicate is that a particular leader may have looked at India and the Indian culture from the point of view of the West and hence therefore, in this we can include starting with Raja Rammohun Roy in the late 19th Century Bengal.

There were two interesting developments.

Ramakrishna Paramahamsa and Vivekananda represented the resurgence of Sanatana Dharma and that in turn inspired people like Golwalkar and others who shaped the course of RSS. Narendra Modi as an active lifelong member of the RSS perhaps feels a particular resonance with the life and preaching of Vivekananda. Because both have the same first name – Narendra (Dutta) and Narendra (Modi).

This inspiration I guess is the fountain spring of all the energy, vision, laser like concentration of mind and a firm sense of commitment to the Vedic invocations for good conduct *Satyam Vada, Dharmam Chara* which have transformed him into a new shining star of today's Indian political firmament. He is distinctly different from all other leaders and is unique.

He decisively stands out from the crowd of selfish, corrupt and opportunistic amoral set of leaders who clutter the political scene today.

He is so different that his political opponents could never guess how leading a party which was not present in one-third of the country, Narendra Modi could manage the miracle of getting a majority in the Lok Sabha for the BJP alone.

I have been writing a fortnightly column in *Bureaucracy Today* from 2012 and this period covers a significant period in Indian politics.

This was a period of an inflection point or tipping point in Indian politics. The Congress-led UPA was in power in Government of India from 2004 to 2014 for a one long decade. Unfortunately, this decade also witnessed a continuous fall in standards of governance. Brazen corruption had become the order of the day. Scam followed scam – CWG, Spectrum, Coal.... The years witnessed a very effective vigorous mobilisation of the civil society groups and the emergence of a totally new phenomenon like Arvind Kejriwal and AAP (Aam Aadmi Party).

Being in power for long time, the Indian National Congress (INC) had slipped into the trap of complacency. INC gradually came to believe that it was the natural party for governance. The opposition parties were too many and too divided regionally and caste identity-based parties. So long a politician was in the INC, he can loot as much of public money as he wanted. Corruption could be blatant and brazen.

These fortnightly pieces have certain features. (i) They deal with one particular problem of the day in all the angles (360 degree) and also try to suggest an effective solution without ever compromising on the principles of ethics in public life. Reading these articles serially as they appeared over the years can help one to understand how the Indian political Right established its credibility and emerged as a viable and ready alternative to the traditional Left which had a long history going back to the freedom struggle and all that followed continuously in the last 60 years of India's independence. Nevertheless, merely reading of these articles in series may not help one to crystallise finally what is the core of the Rightist philosophy and also what are the fountain springs of its contents.

Through out my life also I have followed the inspiration of the *Gita* in Chapter 5. Nevertheless, from my perch, I can appreciate the approach of the rationalists like the Communists and also the arguments of the Dravidian movements. They used to call themselves as rationalists (*pagutharivu vadi*) and quote American atheist Robert Ingersoll. But in their personal life as was clearly brought out by Kannadasan, who is an excellent Tamil poet who deserves to be rated next to only the Subramania Bharathiyar in Tamil, experienced in his life both as an atheist in the Dravidian movement and earlier a great devotee of God, following especially the Kanchi Paramacharya as his Guru. In his book *Arthamulla Indhu Madham*, Kannadasan has exposed the hollowness of the Dravidian movement. So far as his personal life is concerned, his two books, *Manavasam* and *Vanavasam* bring out the spiritual experience and the dawning of enlightenment and wisdom in his own life.

That brings us to the basic question: what is the core of the Indian Right? A lot of criticism from the current leftist establishment intelligentsia which had ruled the roost from the days of independence in 1947 for the last seven decades has projected RSS as a fascist party inspired by the universally condemned villain Adolf Hitler of Germany who committed the horrors of the Holocaust. Insofar as this government is concerned, as mentioned earlier, Narendra Modi is an unabashed but a sincere, ideal member of the Rashtriya Swayamsevak Sangh. What is it that makes the RSS so distinct and so different from the so-called communal organisation? As I see it, these are the distinguishing features of RSS:

> Inspiration for RSS is our Sanatana Dharma. As articulated by Vivekananda in the late 19th century, this represents the quintessence of the Vedanta. The essence of Vedanta has been condensed and articulated lucidly by Swami A Parthasarathy as consisting of just two concepts:
>
> (i) *Atmano Mokshartham* and
>
> (ii) *Jagat Hitaya Cha*.
>
> In essence it means that as an individual, one should try to move towards *moksha* or liberation. Secondly, as a member of the human race, one should contribute to the welfare of the society. In fact, while one focuses on ones spiritual development, one is not expected to be totally aloof from the society but work along with it for the welfare of the society. RSS and earlier Vivekananda himself demonstrated very effectively in their life both these

principles. When Ramakrishna Paramahamsa was approached by Vivekananda, who asked him, "have you seen God?" The Great Master told calmly, "yes, I have seen God as I see you and I can also make you see Him." Then Ramakrishna Paramahamsa touched Narendra Dutta who later on became Vivekananda, there was a spiritual experience called *diksha*, on a transmission of the spiritual power. The disciple experienced the special condition called *Nirvikalpa Samadhi*. This is a state where an individual soul feels one with God. This can be only experienced and not described.

Swami Sukhananda who started a movement called Annalakshmi catering services in Coimbatore used to say that reading all the spiritual literature like *Gita* or Veda is like reading a Railway Guide. It is not the same as undertaking a railway journey.

We come to the next aspect of *atmano mokshartham jagat hitaya cha*. The most important aspect of life which is the essence of Sanatana Dharma and which is absorbed, practised and visible to all is the dedication of helping others. It is here that RSS have established their unique track record of service. In every disaster that takes place in the country, RSS volunteers are the first to be on the scene and help in the process of relief and rehabilitation. This is recognised even by the cynical secular crowd of hostile selfish persons and the political parties. Historically, when Sardar Patel himself noticed that in the post-partition riots, it was the RSS which displayed courage, discipline and selfless help to all victims of the riots to certain extent they were invited to participate in the Republic Day parade in 1949. Reading the writings of Guruji

Golwalkar, one can find that the ideal RSS *pracharak* is supposed to be totally selfless. In fact, the RSS may be appealing to human idealists who help them even at the cost of their life themselves. Do such people exist in reality? Why? Even Jawaharlal Nehru after the disastrous war with China in 1962, 1963, honoured the participation of RSS in the Republic Day parade.

Quite a few RSS *pracharakas* are unmarried and devote their life to total service. Is it possible to display altruism of hurting oneself? Interestingly, in the Christmas double issue of the London-based *The Economist* magazine for 2015, there is a review of a book called *Strangers Drowning: Grappling with Impossible Idealism, Drastic Choices and the Overpowering Urge to Help* by Larissa MacFarquhar. I reproduce the entire piece in full to bring out that such people also exist who are so altruistic to the extent of not caring for their own interest. All of us are familiar with the concept of enlightened self-interest. But this is something different but not impossible.

> "The do-gooder", writes Larissa MacFarquhar in *Strangers Drowning* "sets out to live as ethical a life as possible." This is the kind of person who has himself injected with the leprosy bacillus to be a subject for medical testing, or who drives hundreds of miles after a hurricane to save factory-farm chickens. Do-gooders have flocked to Greece to help refugees.
>
> In a series of character studies-coupled into his eccentric and intriguing book with historical and philosophical essays Ms MacFarquhar profiles a range of do-gooders including an Indian aristocrat, a Bostonian social worker and a Japanese monk. These disparate

altruists are united by the priority they place on the duty to help strangers. They are moral above all else, suppressing desires, sacrificing pleasures and often enduring years of loneliness. The saviour of chickens believes that advocating for chickens' rights is the best way for him to reduce worldwide suffering. "He wasn't interested in happiness," the author writes. "He was interested in pain."

Ms MacFarquhar is a staff writer at *The New Yorker*. She is a careful expositor of ideas. *Strangers Drowning*, a defence of the authenticity of do gooders, presents an exemplary subject for a writer who is at once cerebral and anecdotal, critical and sympathetic.

Ms MacFarquhar does not argue that saintly behaviour is simply a question of doing one's duty. Instead, she sets out to prove that altruists are not necessarily deluded or dispirited. And she uses her distinctive profiler's tone to show, as she puts it, "the beauty and cost of a certain kind of moral existence". For Ms MacFarquhar's subjects themselves, everyone is morally obliged to be maximally good all the time, and anything less is unjustifiably selfish. Many critics, on the other hand, find such moralising fanatical and perverse. Do-gooders are often not especially likeable. One tells his girlfriend he will not clean up after himself because "time spent washing dishes could be time spent working for animal rights". They are distrusted by those who suspect that hidden motives underlie their goodness. Ms MacFarquhar refers to doctors who have called kidney donors 'screwballs', 'abnormal' and 'not to be trusted'.

Susan Wolf, a philosopher whose landmark essay 'Moral Saints', is a foil for Ms MacFarquhar's thinking, has argued that moral perfectionism and personal well-being are incompatible. Because "morality itself doesn't seem to be a suitable object of passion," moral saints must either lack or repress the amoral desires that give people their humanity, Susan Wolf writes.

That view might seem intuitively correct to anyone who aspires to virtues that are not moral in nature – who would, for example, act immorally for a friend in need. If morality forbids all partiality and self-cultivation, any special attachment to friends and family, even to yourself – then people may well question whether it is good to be moral. Ms MacFarquhar is not endorsing the strict moral requirements upheld by her subjects. She does, however, refute. Ms Wolf's claim that do-gooders must be robots or hypocrites. Many are motivated by uncommon moral sentiments. *Strangers Drowning* begins with a vignette in which a young philosophy student is reduced to tears merely by reflecting on the existence of suffering.

Even the most self-sacrificial do-gooders can achieve a remarkable clarity and contentment. One couple adopts 20 children, many of whom end up in prison, have unwanted pregnancies or die young. But the whole family remains close inspite of it all. "Their days were crowded and unpredictable," writes the author, "and charged with fervour and purpose." These do-gooders could be described as moral overachievers, an unlikely group whose well-being can consist in extreme moral goodness, whose partiality itself seems impartial. Concluding that their behaviour is nor morally required does not dismiss the challenges they present. Readers of this book will question whether they can admire do-gooders while wishing to be nothing like them."

This I think is the distinguishing feature of RSS compared to other so-called secular, rational parties and communists. At best, we can concede that every person has a self-interest but we can sublimate the entire thing to what can be called sublimation of the private interest into public interest. But it is the unique feature of the RSS what I would call the Indian political Right based on Sanatana Dharma that it tries to reach out to the type of cases highlighted by Larissa MacFarquhar.

That brings us in short, to the two core principles of the Indian Right.

The first is supreme patriotism looking upon one's own country as mother.

The second is the dedication to serve living up to the Vedantic principle of *atmano mokshartham jagat hitaya cha – paropakaram idam shareeram* is the other well-known statement articulating the above principle. Secular parties as a Hindu communal party, BJP in fact fights for the soil. BJP is severely hounded by Hinduism.

That brings us to the third important aspect of BJP or the Indian political Right namely, Hinduism. Hinduism has never been a religion based on a single book of unchangeable truth. It is not like the Semitic religions like Judaism, Christianity and Islam. Compared to other religions, it has survived millions of years because of its capacity for adjusting to the environment and transforming itself. Dinosaurs died but smaller mammals survived because they could adjust to the changing environment and did not suffer what is called as the boiled frog syndrome. You can keep the frog in a bowl of water and gradually increase the temperature. Ultimately, the frog is not aware of the changes taking place and could be boiled to death. Hindu religion based on Sanatana Dharma never suffered from this weakness because, it has always been opened to new ideas and changes. An ancient Vedic Rigveda invocation says, *anobhadraha kritavo yantu vishwatah*, let noble thoughts come to us from every side. Mahatma Gandhi articulated the same thing when he said, "I want to keep my windows of culture open but do not want to be blown off the feet."

In short, the Indian political Right is based on the very sound principle namely our tradition, our concept of Sanatana Dharma and attachment to the principle of *dharma.* Other political ideology may fail in the long run because they don't have a sound ethical basis and also a reasonable approach. That is because Hinduism and Sanatana Dharma in the ultimate analysis are supremely logical and entirely coherent philosophy. Therefore, it is said that Hinduism is not a religion; Sanatana Dharma is a way of life.

In the current context, Narendra Modi and his colleagues are trying to usher in the era of a viable, modern and vigorous Indian Political Right rooted in the sound principles of Sanatana Dharma.

The vigour with which the India Right has at last been able to bring up to tectonic change in the Indian political scene so far as the philosophy of government is concerned, springs from a number of sources rooted in our ancient Indian culture and Sanatana Dharma.

An interesting aspect of Sanatana Dharma is that it prescribes values and code of conduct for every aspect of life. It helps one to achieve excellence in skills combined with sound ethics. Sanatana Dharma helps in achieving this. That is the special aspect of political Right.

I have the advantage of having lived a full life. I am familiar with at least six languages, Marathi, Gujarati, Hindi, Tamil, Sanskrit and English. I joined the IAS in 1960 when the first Prime Minister of India Jawaharlal Nehru was very much active and leading the nation. I have had a full innings of 42 years in public administration; I could appreciate the dynamics of the Indian political life, particularly public life and governance.

The concept of good governance at last has become familiar to at least those leadership levels in the politics of India. Even those who are aware of essential features of good governance, find themselves helpless because they find themselves in a situation where the idealism of our fathers and grandfathers for independence from the British has evaporated. There is no clear philosophy other than the denatured idealism of the leftist philosophy which so fascinated Jawaharlal Nehru.

The vigour of the political Right comes from two factors. One is familiarity with and acceptance of the fact that India's culture has been shaped by thousands of years of Sanatana Dharma whose basic feature is as articulated by Swami Parthasarathy, *atmano mokshartham jagat hitaya cha.* As individuals, we aspire to move towards liberation or freedom from the eternal cycle of birth and death. At the same time, we have not to spend our life in this earth only looking to the other world. As human beings on earth, we have a duty to ensure that whatever time we have on this earth we work for the benefit and welfare of all people in the earth.

The world itself is visualised as one large family, *vasudhaiva kutumbakam* and in the acceptance of the fact that it is not only the humans alone who are important but every form of life ranging from the plants to animals, flora and fauna are equally to be respected. They have their presence in this earth and they deserve their presence and we should love all those creations of God.

In the earlier sections, we had seen how this quintessence of this Sanatana Dharma evolved thanks to a very unique combination of various factors raising from the geological, astronomical as well as biological needs, where the concept of equality and the inter-connectivity of all forms of life not only realised but consciously emphasised in different forms and practised. So the foundation for the India's potential Right is more ancient and has been time tested.

Unlike the Leftist philosophy which perhaps goes back to the industrial revolution of not more than 300 to 400 years.

Secondly, the Leftist philosophy is based on the concept that the imperatives of Darwinism dictate our behaviour as human beings. When it comes to life, it is the survival of the fittest when it comes to matters like organisations, commercial institutions, it is again the same approach of survival of the fittest. When the competition gets tough and there is no level playing field and their arises powerful regulator in the form of a State or a Monarch. Then this very selfishness gets sublimated to what could be called enlightened self-interest. It becomes the *raison d'être* of laws and regulations of a well-ordered society.

The traditional Indian business class like the Marwaris and the Gujaratis, and Chettiars believe in the principle that while they will conduct their business according to the laws prevailing under the State, they will also try to follow their Vaishya Dharma of ensuring that they are able to create wealth by hook or crook. This is justified, I have heard many businessmen say that they may do a number of things which technically may violate laws and may be considered as crimes or breach of law, but they will never violate the laws made by God. What they called laws made by God are the ancient principles and directives that have been crystallised insofar as Hindus are concerned, in our *Vedas, Upanishads, Subhashitas* and *Niti Shastra.* This concept of *neeyat* or intention of not having any *mens rea* has been brought out by an outstanding modern manager, Gopalakrishnan, who had a long innings in Tatas and also now become an author. His very first book *The Case of the Bonsai Manager*, highlights with his background experience in the Middle-East. He points out how ultimately, the value of any good business is in the *neeyat* or intention. Tatas have built an enormous reputation as an ethical company for more than century from the time of Jamsetji Nusserwanji Tata set up the steel factory about ethics I have had opportunity to witness first-hand how Tatas go to great extent to inculcate the spirit of ethics in the Tatas values in every employee of that great organisation.

The fundamental point where the right of the centre as articulated and represented by Narendra Modi and the RSS from which he hails is that this emphasis and attachment to religion and Sanatana Dharma. The concept of *dharma* is not only restricted to religion, but every aspect of human activity. In the case of Left for example, business is purely an economic activity, politics is purely a game of exercising power and competing for advantage. Peter Drucker, the management guru says that purpose of business is to create a customer and retain him. The purpose of politics as an extrapolation of the Peter Drucker concept of business would be to grab power and retain it. As long as this basic *raison d'être* of politics and business are achieved, from the ideological point of view, the Left is satisfied.

It is the additional attachment to the concept of *dharma* or values which gives vigour and long-time sustainability to the Indian political Right. As many may not be aware of this link, I thought it will be worthwhile to highlight specific points, even though once articulated, it may appear to be so banal and so obvious. The interesting aspect of wisdom in life is that once any concept is explained, it looks so simple, banal and transparent and obvious.

Thanks to the legacy of Nehruvian socialism and its extrapolation in politics in the form of secularism, as articulated in the Constitution, the establishment intelligentsia of today is not able to appreciate the tectonic change in the shift which Narendra Modi has brought so far as the ideology of governance is concerned. At the moment, they are still in a state of shock and in a mood of denial.

Two years out of the five year term of Modi is over. All the time, they, I am afraid, have still not understood the roots of vigour Modi's Rightist philosophy. Modi government's philosophy looks likely to emerge ultimately in the long run as the second party of governance. In every democracy, there are parties of the Left and the Right and the movement is always towards the centre. Unless any of the ruling party has the necessary internal flexibility and toughness to move towards the centre without giving up its core values, then no vigorous political party for governance can exist. So far as India is concerned, thanks to historical factors, Indian National Congress has evolved as a major pole of politics and the parties who are in tune with that philosophy normally brands themselves as secular parties and belong to that pole. The opposite pole is represented by Modi and RSS. For a long time, the Left was under the complacent view that however much Modi may try to aspire to become the Prime Minister, he cannot succeed because his party did not exist in a third of the country.

The miracle has happened in the 2014 elections. Modi achieved a majority in the parliament, thanks to the vigour which arises from the BJP's close link of religion, values and the Sanatana Dharma. Unlike the Left which tend to either brand the entire BJP as a communal party or some of them extreme elements or loonies, there is a large core of educated leaders with BJP. Fortunately many of them are in the government ranging from Narendra Modi, Arun Jaitley and the senior ministers in the cabinet who are the effective ministers of the vigour of the rightist philosophy.

*Ramayana* and *Mahabharata* are known all over India. I would go to the extent of saying that India is wherever *Ramayana* and *Mahabharata* are known and respected. These epics are part of our conventional wisdom. Knowledge about these epics is a sure indication of the Indian culture. This is because *Ramayana* and *Mahabharata* are not merely religious epics but they represent the quintessence of good governance. Gurucharan Das very much a product of today's globalized world brought it out beautifully in his book, "The difficulty of being good", his interpretation of *Mahabharata*. In this book, he took certain incidents from the *Mahabharata* and related them to modern India Inc philosophies. Coming from a person who has been very much in the heart of globalized multinational companies, he points out how the issue of *neeyat* is tackled. I have already mentioned about Gopalakrishnan of the Tatas. *Ramayana* and *Mahabharata* are popular with the people in our country because over thousands of years, there have been storytellers who have been entertaining people and through entertainment, they not only capable tradition of our faith but also brought out the fundamental principles of good conduct both in personal life and in public life.

One of the great features of Chennai is the music season. The music season is not merely an opportunity to enjoy or immerse oneself in the great tradition of Carnatic music but also its various dimensions. In *The Hindu*, Chennai issue of 15th January 2016, which happens to be the most auspicious festival of Tamil Nadu, called Pongal, a major feature brings out a link between the ancient tradition of *Kathakalakshepam* and the modern youth. This is because, some of the very educated youth like engineers who studied in IITs and BITS, Pilani and Chartered Accountants have turned to propagating the traditional form of music like *Kathakalakshepam.* I reproduce the highlights of that article, about three artists, Vishaka Hari, Dushyanth Sridhar and Suchithra.

> "The bravest battle that ever was fought:
>
> Shall I tell you where and when? On the maps of the world you will find it not: It was fought by the mothers of men.
>
> Vishaka Hari recites these lines from American poet Joaquin Miller's 'Motherhood' at a Harikatha performance this season. She is explaining the Vedic maxim 'Matru devo

bhava' as being not just about the umbilical bond but also the passion with which men like Bhagat Singh fought and gave up their lives for the motherland.

"Harikatha," says this chartered accountant, "is not simply narration of a *katha*. It is exploring the many angles to a thought. It is a seamless blend of music, drama, literature, history, philosophy and science."

Harikatha, a folk form with its roots in Maharashtra, first gained popularity in Thanjavur where the Marathas settled in large numbers. Practitioners would stand in the middle of the stage as they told stories, sang, danced, and played instruments.

Harikatha artists today perform sitting down, not all of them sing and none dance. But they have yet widened the appeal of their art with refreshing new approaches.

"I connect as deeply with the characters in my stories as Harry Potter fans do with the tales spun by JK Rowling," laughs Dushyanth Sridhar, chemical engineer-turned-*upanyasakar*. Talking on his way back from delivering a lecture at a school, where he drew links between Krishna, calculus, history and geography, he says the effort is to create relevance and realistic associations.

He video-records each performance and uploads them on YouTube. "These videos are movie teasers to get the attention of the social media generation. I don't want to be preachy, but I want them to realise that Harikatha is not just for the old; there's a lot that youngsters can take from it," he says.

This season, Dushyanth's performance included a Katha-Natyam with Bharatanatyam dancer Ramya Ramnarayan and a Katha-Kutcheri with vocalists Carnatica Brothers.

"Like every other art, it offers enough scope for creative experiments."

Having grown up listening to Beatles and Harry Belafonte, Dushyanth's foray in to the art of Kathakalakshepam was accidental, when he was asked by a professor at BITS Pilani to talk on the *Ramayana* because of his knowledge of Sanskrit. "My mother had enrolled me in Sanskrit class during my school days in Bangalore as she thought it would help me learn languages. I would also accompany my grandparents sometimes to Harikatha performances. But I never imagined that I would one day take it up myself. My professor, I think, was the trigger."

Sudha Seshayyan brings the probing mind of a doctor to her discourses and researches for thematic productions. A medical professor, her lucid explanations of the various aspects of the scriptures and texts seem a result of her methodical study of the human mind and body.

She attributes Harikatha's growing popularity to the way in which texts are deconstructed, the logic and reasoning in narration, and the ability to establish a connect with changing audiences. Also, as Harikatha artists collaborate now with dancers and vocalists, they create effective ways to help audiences understand the lyrics and relate to the emotions. All of them weave in contemporary issues and references into the tales from the epics, Upanishads and Puranas.

For Carnatic vocalist B Suchithra, what started as the upkeep of the legacy has become an exciting way of reaching out to people, especially young people. "This Season," she says, "I met an 18-year-old boy from California who said he had

> been attending Harikatha performances to understand its nuances. When abroad, I have even given discourses in English. After all, it's about sharing and being understood."
>
> Granddaughter of veteran Harikatha exponent Thanjavur RR Kamala Murthy, Suchithra was in the second year of her Commerce degree when she gave her first performance.
>
> From the days when venerable Bhagavathars held village squares in thrall through long moonlit nights to the floodlit and savvy performance of these modern-day raconteurs, Kathakalakshepam has shown that storytelling will always survive. All it needs is a twist to the tale."

The above analysis shows that in releasing *Ramayana, Mahabbharata* of intense interest in them does not necessarily mean a backward looking, traditional, conservative Hindu but also a person who has a double advantage for having strong foundation for moral behaviour and at the same time aware of the constant features for ethical governance.

In fact, Norman Vincent Peale and Kenneth Blanched wrote a short book of 131 pages called *Power of Ethical Management*. There is a three point test they prescribed for deciding over whether a decision is ethical. (i) Is it legal? (ii) Is it fair? And (iii) Is the action is such, if it becomes public knowledge, it will embarrass everyone. To understand this concept better, one can recall the standard joke about the 11th commandment of the Bible. Bible has only 10 commandments. But it is said that there is an 11th commandment which is not there in the Bible but if one observes the 11th commandment, one can violate all the 10th commandments. What is the 11th commandment, 'thou shall not be found out'. Today in these days of IT everywhere and in the digital age, Anna Hazare have proved that the political leaders cannot get away bluffing by practising hypocrisy. It is this aspect of the media exposure which has emerged as an important aspect which will bring discipline among the truly important political leader so that they don't manage to cheat people and the aspect of corruption can be effectively tackled.

While this much may be obvious, there is another aspect of Puranas and other traditional moral tales that help manage a large multinational company with Indian management to build up a family spirit of a long time survival. Kishore Biyani of Big Bazaar seems to have grasped this basic principle. He has appointed Patnaik as a religion advisor or spiritual advisor for the Company and Patnaik has been particularly articulate in magazine about spelling out how mythology helps in drawing the right conclusion and approach. In short, the Rightist's philosophy is based in religion have a double advantage. Not only that it helps to perpetuate values or develop the vision of the world as a family, but also through the moral lessons from the past stories create opportunities for modern managers in global companies to undertake an exercise in lateral thinking to find solutions. This is exactly what Gurcharan Das was trying to do in his book *The Difficulty of Being Good: On the Subtle Art of Dharma*. *Mahabharata* or *Bhagawad Gita* for example are excellent guides for finding solutions to problems in politics and Modi leading the Right of Centre government has therefore come fully prepared for five years of power and it looks that he will continue to win and prove historic mark on the democratic evolution of India. As of now, the first two years established his credentials in the world. The third year 2016 was the one, where the focus was on the domestic issues. Coming two years are such that automatically more and more attention will be focused on the approach of elections and should be geared to that end. Having demonstrated decisively in 2014 that with the tools available and the vision derived from Sanatana Dharma a party can capture power and he may go on to prove once again that as in the United States, there are spells where for certain decades, the Democratic Part is in power and then comes a transition, then for the next two decades or so, the Republican's rule. We can expect a similar development to take place in India also as it matures in to a real vigorous well-governed democracy.

There is yet another advantage on this dependence and link with mythologies and Puranas. As the entire population is aware of this background, any political comparisons or reference to the Puranas and mythologies is a surest way of ensuring that the false of the political leaders are universally understood by the public. After all, communication is the most important aspect in politics. Mahatma Gandhi did it very famously in the Salt Satyagraha and his great achievement was to convert the Indian National Congress which till that time was only a party of the elite meeting in rich surroundings and polite resolutions for consideration by the British government.

Ultimately, India became independent because the people of the country could no longer tolerate the British rule. As the French intellectual Alexis de Tocqueville observed in the context of American Revolution, **the inevitable becomes the intolerable, the moment it is perceived to be no more inevitable.** There was a situation in the late 19th century but after bitter experiences under the then prevailing order of rulers and decaying Mogul empire and the adventures of the Marathas, the people had come to accept the British rule, even though that of a foreigner as the best of the lot and at the beginning of the 20th century, it appeared that Queen Victoria in her glory could roll over an empire over which sun never set. From that situation to create awareness among the people of India who were mostly illiterate in an era where the communication facilities are hardly as good of as today in the 21st century, Gandhiji was able to rely on the roots of Indian tradition and culture to awaken the masses and make them realise that the British Rule was not inevitable. The moment it is perceived to be inevitable, it became intolerable and what followed is the history through which we are living.

Biyani and Patnaik in running Big Bazaar have realised that even in a business environment, which has got global and multinational aspects, the link with mythology helps for effective communication within the organisation outside.

Apart from the communication so far as the public are concerned, another dimension is communication within the government itself. Here the standard expressions of *Subhashitas* Vedic quotations and similar proverbs play a very important role. For instance, the importance of truth is emphasised but at the same time, there is also guidance that the truth must not be sugar coated. One of the *Subhashitas* says, *satyam bruyat priyam bruyat na bruyat satyam apriyam* and then there is the Mundakopanishad lesson which has been adopted as the motto of the Government of India *Satyamev Jayate,* a full version goes – *satyamev jayate man rytham* and nothing else stands. The only point not indicated is how much time it takes for the truth to prevail and it is where a lot of discussion takes place in the media about the delays in our judicial system. Justice delayed is justice denied is another well-known expression. Is it possible to have good governance by ensuring justice which is quick and at the same time *dharmic*. The challenge before the political right represented by Narendra Modi is to achieve this and this in turn starts with modernisation of administration for which lot of measures have already been initiated. The digital India is one such initiative. It is embracing of technology by the right of centre Modi may prima facie look oxymoron but the very fact that a leader like Modi sleeked in organisation like RSS, which talks about Sanatana Dharma is open to embracing modern ideas is easily understood if one goes in to the fact that Sanatana Dharma has never been opposed to having open mind. In fact, it is this which gives the call for let our noble thoughts come to us from every side. *Aano bhadra krtavo yantu vishwatah*.

The Hinduism prescribes to question everything and then accept it based on rational analysis and for deriving knowledge, there are many ancient books which show the right path. Thiruvalluvar, the saint Tamil Nadu in Thirukkural talks about how one should not believe whatever one says but subject everything to whatever the nature and whatever the source of the statement should be examined – *Epporul yaryar vai ketpinum apporul meiporul kanbathu arivu*.

At the same time, the respect for the teachers is also very much emphasised in the *Bhagawad Gita* in Chapter 6. How *shishyas* should learn from the Guru.

Thiruvalluvar even more direct in

*Udayar mun illarpol ekkathum katrar kadayare kallathavar*

Like a poor beggar begging before a rich man, *shishya* should adopt the attitude placing himself in the position of a beggar and approach a guru as a rich man who can pass on the wealth to him and survive. But in the learning process also, it is not a blind learning. The learning should be after analysis. *Tat bhudhi paripartena pari preshnena shevayam*. *Prari prartena* talks about raising question and also analysis. In Sanatana Dharma has anticipated and looked into all aspects for learning and in these days of modern technology, Modi has rightly focused on Make in India and Skill India.

These initiatives also show that the foundation for good governance based on a right of centre philosophy is the lead. Apparently, the critics of Modi cannot appreciate these aspects as they are still in a word of denial. So far as the economic development policies are concerned, the attitude of total hostility and non-cooperation are displayed in the Rajya Sabha by the Congress shows how limited has become their mission.

Incidentally, there is yet another aspect of technology, when it comes to good governance and inclusive growth so far as our country is concerned. *The Hindu* dated 15th January 2016 has an article by Shubhranshu Choudhary titled 'Techtonic for the Heart of India'. It points out that the Gondi is the lingua franca of the Maoist movement but All India Radio does not broadcast even a single news bulletin in the language.

> "One winter morning, in Barwani district of Madhya Pradesh, I was watching a group of Adivasi kids peering into their mobile phones. The early morning sun was mellow, and they were so engrossed that they did not notice me drawing near.
>
> "We are doing Bultoo sir," one of them told me when I asked what they were doing.

It took me some time to understand that they were transferring audio and video files using Bluetooth technology in their mobile phones.

I was in Barwani to take a class on citizen journalism with Adivasi children.

Later, I discovered that more than 80% of the students had Bluetooth in their mobile phones and actively used it to share audio and video files with each other. I had no idea that even my mobile phone is Bluetooth-enabled. I had never used it. On the other end of Central India, in Balrampur district, on the border of Chhattisgarh and Jharkhand, I found a similar phenomenon. It is a Maoist insurgency-affected district with a large proportion of Oraon tribals, who speaks a language called Kuduk. An experiment here has thrown up a model for how to solve the problem.

Eighty per cent of Balarampur's Gram Panchayats are connected by optical fibre cables thanks to the Digital India push by Prime Minister Narendra Modi.

The problem is, there is broadband but there isn't much content in Kuduk on the Internet.

If wages under the Mahatma Gandhi National Rural Employment Guarantee Act (MGNREGA) haven't been paid, if forest right deeds have not been distributed, they report about it in Kuduk. Once the messages get recorded on a central computer connected via the Internet, they also get translated into Hindi and English. Then, the messages reach officers such as Collector Alex Paul Menon, who was once abducted by the Maoists, and also reach each Gram Panchayat. One person from each village comes to the

Gram Panchayat office every day and downloads the daily programme of 'Bultoo Radio' on his mobile phone and shares it with all villages upon return.

'Bultoo Radio' is a small experiment being carried out over a small area but its problem-solving potential and its use of the local idiom can bring people's faith back in the system. Something similar can also be done with short-wave radio, which people here tune into to listen to programmes broadcast by Evangelical Christian groups based in places such as the Philippines. Balrampur has Internet in most of its Gram Panchayats but Dantewada doesn't in even 1% of its Panchayats – 'Bultoo Radio' will not work there, but short wave will.

The Maoist problem is basically a problem of communication breakdown while Maoists, missionaries, mining companies reach out to the Adivasis, mainstream India remains blissfully cocooned. There are no officers, no journalists who understand Adivasi languages such as Kuduk, Gondi. The Maoists did not come to the Dandakaranya forests to effect a revolution, they came here to hide. Despite the Maoists interacting and working with Adivasis for 40 years in the region, there are hardly any Adivasi Maoist leaders. At any rate, less than 1% of the Maoists in Central India use violence as a tool to change politics; 99% of them have been sold an illusion that once their 'Raj' comes, all their problems will be solved, the problems of forest, land, water, health and education.

India needs to have two strategies to solve the Maoist problem, one for Maoists and one for Maoist supporters who make it "India's biggest internal security threat."

On other hand, thanks to the technology revolution, the Naxals have got mobile phone and they are using the Bluetooth technology to communicate among themselves and coordinate their movements against the government. There could be two uses about the muscular Hinduism advocated by RSS and such organisations based on what is branded as Hindutva. In fact, the behaviour of two great Shankaracharyas of the Kanchi Kamakoti Peetha in the last century brought out the two diametrically opposite approaches to 'defending Hinduism'. Paramacharya, the senior one, perhaps took the view that Hindu Sanatana Dharma has proved by its track record of thousands of year that it can sustain itself against the worst of criticism, atheism and all the might of the State that can be arraigned against it. He therefore, scrupulously avoided making any comment about the aggressive Dravidian movement and earlier Justice Party movement in the early part of 20th century. Even when the Dravidian Party came to power, he maintained his stand. His disciple, eminent Jayendra Saraswathi, who is now the senior Shankaracharya, took the stand that action was needed to meet the challenge of non-Hindu religions like Islam and Christianity. He therefore, initiated the process of Jankalyan and tried to meet the challenge of the Semitic religions. He described his difference with his guru on the ground that while the Paramacharya represent the *Iccha Shakti*, he represented the *Kriya Shakti*. Between *pravritti* and *nivritti*, Paramacharya chose *nivritti* and Jayendra Saraswathi chose *pravritti*. But this was not a single, exceptional development. In the past, there have been in the streams of Vaishnavism and Shaivism, Veera Vaishnavas and Veera Shaivas, very strong movements like the Lingayats in Karnataka and so on. In the Mughal times, Sikhism itself became almost shield of Hinduism from the extremist stand adopted by rulers like Aurangzeb.

At the end of the day, Sanatana Dharma has remained as the main spiritual binding force of our great nation Bharatavarsha.

These articles published in the *Bureaucracy Today* every month from 2012 are grouped in to four categories so that one can appreciate how the tectonic change Modi has been able to bring about in the Indian political scene evolved, works and its long-term future. As brought out in the introduction, the echoes of more or less every concept would be also traced in these articles. But the articles examine the concept in some depths which may not be possible in a comprehensive introduction, which can at best provide only an overall view and the inter-connectivity.

The articles are grouped under the following categories:

(i) The shift to the Right itself. This tackles issues relating to operational problems raised at the time of the shift Right from the earlier days of the government and the attitude of the opposition and the media reflecting the resistance of the established and Left of centre intelligentsia.

(ii) The new actions of the Right government, especially in areas like Defence and National Security and foreign relations.

(iii) 'Good governance' explores the implementation of the agenda of the Right, so that one can see how Modi has not only been able to steer the shift of politics to the Right but also laying the foundation for a long-term presence of the Right of centre as a viable alternative to the Left of centre in Indian politics, which had driven the first 70 years of India's independence.

For seventy years since independence governing philosophy of the Government of India, largely influenced by Jawaharlal Nehru and the leaders of the freedom struggle was distinctly to the left of the centre and totally disconnected from the values of Sanatana Dharma. This development ignored the basic fact that a long-term view of India's evolution and the inspiration for such governance, was denied from the eternal teachings of Sanatana Dharma. This spiritual form was universally known as Bharatavarsha and Bharata Khanda, thanks to a number of tenable factors. The focus on left of centre and complete detachment from the basic roots of national consciousness of us as the children of Bharatavarsha was in a sense an artificial temporary aberration. A badly needed corrective has now been provided thanks to the enormous initiative and the drive and as well as the leadership shown by Narendra Modi and the results of 2014 elections. The question is whether as the establishment intelligentsia of today bred over the last seventy years with government patronage will succeed in halting this well-needed corrective. In my judgement, Narendra Modi has started on the right lines both on the policy and programme implementation. He rightly emphasised during the election campaign not so much on the religious aspect or Hindutva, but on the needs of good governance. At the same time, he also continuously highlighted the need for cleanliness in public life. The disconnect with the ethical dimension was the great weakness of left of centre governance. The UPA-II government which recorded a history of scandals provided the perfect foil for Narendra Modi to project his alternative vision. This combined with the appeal to the roots of Indian culture and Indian consciousness apparently led to the tectonic shift to the political right. In the articles I wrote to the *Bureaucracy Today*, I have tried to point out how many of the ideas of Narendra Modi are not only in tune with the basic philosophy of the Sanatana Dharma but also at the same time are eminently pragmatic and doable. Even 'Namami Gange' project which prima facie may appear to be a lost cause can be realised in our life time. This inspite of the fact that more than 30 years, ` 30,000 crore have been spent by different governments on this project.

This is because for this government and Modi, Ganga is not merely a river; it is something sacred and innately connected with our Bharatiya consciousness. Anyone who has read Jawaharlal Nehru's *Discovery of India* will realise that even for a thoroughly westernised intellectual like Jawaharlal Nehru, Ganga had its unique appeal. Perhaps, subliminally, Jawaharlal Nehru as one of the great sons of Bharatavarsha realised the significance of Ganga representing the cultural essence of this country. As mentioned earlier, the articles which I wrote in the *Bureaucracy Today* have been classified for the sake of convenience and coherence into four categories. The first relates to articulating the essential spirit and soul of what constitutes India's political Right and its close association with patriotism and national pride. The realisation that mother country is dearer than heaven. *Janani janma bhumisya sokathathesya hegarishtati*, means that as children of Bharatmata, we should be alert all the time for our national service and defence. The new approach to Defence articulated by the current government perfectly in tune with this significance of the core of India's political right. The other two parts deal with more pragmatic issues of governance. Bulk of these articles relate to governance. Our constitution says that India is a union of States and not a Federation. The criticism of the Narendra Modi government is against Federalism is not correct. Articles on cooperative federalism show that this concept need not be a mere catch word, but can be a pragmatic policy of finding a new meaning in the working of the Constitution. Both the Government of India and the States can make their own contribution in building up a 21st century India which will be an economic super power.

If for a moment shift our focus and take a longer view of history, we find that there are all in these period of long history of more than ten thousand years we did not whenever the Sanatana Dharma was forgotten and our society deteriorated because it moved away from the principle of Sanatana Dharma, it always found its way back to the main core of its cultural soul, thanks to the timely appearance of the right spiritual leaders as well as political leaders. The founding of our Vijayanagara empire in the 14th century and the case of Samartha Ramdas and Shivaji together in the 17th century immediately come to mind. The same could be considered in the past when there have been great leaders of Vaishnava and Shaiva Sampradaya who have guided the kings and influenced the course of governance for the country. Even in his famous book *The Continent of Circe*, Nirad Chaudhuri, a self-confessed anglophile, identified this unique characteristic of our country already like a snake shred its old skin from time to time and always remould itself, they coming back to its basic culture and its concept of Sanatana Dharma again and again.

In a perceptive article in *The Hindu*, dated 5th February 2016, Suhas Palshikar who teaches political science at the Savitribai Phule Pune University, Pune had analysed the evolution of the governance philosophy of BJP. The article titled 'Modi-Shah Template for the BJP' published in *The Hindu*, dated 4th February 2016, as a half-paged article makes the following interesting comments:

> "In the 10 years after the Godhra riots, Narendra Modi evolved a new model of Hindutva politics. The basis of this model lay in ruthless use of the State apparatus to signal to the minorities where they belonged. Once that was achieved, it was only one step to Hindutva penetrating Gujarati civil society and the popular imagination. Then his focus shifted to improving the macroeconomic performance of the State. The fourth dimension of that model was to focus on the lower middle classes instead of the lower bottom (which was the focus of the Manmohan Singh government at the Centre). The 'Gujarat model' was further augmented by the adoption of an unprecedented and most astute media blitzkrieg. A new BJP was thus born – through the 2007 and 2012 State elections in Gujarat. It travelled to Delhi with Narendra Modi from the time of his speech at Delhi's Shri Ram College of Commerce in early 2013.
>
> ... most fundamentally, for the BJP, which prides in its links with the Rashtriya Swayamsevak Sangh and its espousal of Hindutva, the biggest challenge would be negotiating with its Hindutva ideology. For the past two years, the party is hiding behind the so-called fringe elements. The game plan seems to be that while the

> 'fringe' functions as storm trooper, the party would slowly make Hindutva politically acceptable. It has neither officially moved away from Hindutva nor formally made efforts to position itself as a part of Hindutva."

In fact, if we take the Sanatana Dharma as the core philosophy of India's political right as represented by BJP today, then the following points become obvious:

For a long time RSS has been perceived to be a militant form of Hinduism. Veer Savarkar articulated the concept of Hindutva and the secular intelligentsia had always branded RSS as a fascist organisation adopting Hitler's technique depending on violence. Although, some may describe the very aggressive initiative taken by the RSS as the fringe element, the suspicion has always been articulated as a hidden agenda of the BJP. Even when Atal Bihari Vajpayee was at the helm, he was described by Govindacharya as a *mukhota.* It was said by 'secular' leaders that Atalji was a right leader in a wrong party and so on. On the other hand, when Narendra Modi reached the helm of affairs, the time had become right for openly accepting the enlightened form of Sanatana Dharma, which invariably has been insisted by all great leaders of Hinduism as the essence of Hinduism can be openly articulated as the governing philosophy or ideology of India's political right. Practically all the great spiritual leaders in ancient and recent times have by their behaviour and action shown that Sanatana Dharma is the essence of Hinduism ultimately means that does not need any militant defence. The great Paramacharya of Kanchi Kamakoti Peetham in the 20th century faced the full onslaught of the anti-Brahmin and atheistic movement lead by vociferous leaders like EV Ramasamy Naicker and the Dravida

Kazhagam and the Dravida Munnetra Kazhagam. Over the years, Sanatana Dharma in Tamil Nadu has re-established itself and it is the atheist movement which seems to have lost steam in the last 70 years.

Nevertheless, it was a fact that there have been in Hinduism itself when the clashes between the different schools of thoughts became violent. There are many examples of militant Hinduism in the past. There were sects like Veera Shaivas and Veera Vaishnavas. When faced with hostile rule, like that of the Mughals, Sikhism became the militant defence of Hinduism and there have been other similar movements. But, ultimately, what has remained as a core of Hinduism which has maximum number of followers is the middle of the road of Sanatana Dharma. The RSS drawing inspiration from Vivekananda can easily adopt the significance and long-term blessings of Sanatana Dharma and can continue to survive the organisational support and the role of a mentor for the BJP which is more directly concerned with the political governance of the country.

Finally, a simple point which many may overlook, when it comes to the context of invoking the cultural and spiritual dimension of Sanatana Dharma as the unifying and underlying philosophy for the India's political right. The continuous drum beating about the separation of the Church and the State and the secular socialistic ideology has perhaps made many Indian themselves inheritors of the rich traditions and spiritual heritage of Sanatana Dharma about how Sanatana Dharma and Hinduism are different from other religions. In 21st century, a nation based only on religion will be called a theocratic State. In fact, the partition of India in 1947 and the

Hindu Muslim violence that preceded it was based on the so-called two-nation theory. The liberation of Bangladesh demonstrated once and overall the whole world the fact that religion alone cannot be the binding force for unifying and articulating the identity of a nation. That is where, Sanatana Dharma or Hinduism scores over other religions which do not have its internal vibrancy and time tested intellectual coherence which is a result of more than 5,000 to 7,000 years of history.

As we have seen the Sanatana Dharma inspired and sustained development of skills and also welded with the concept of Dharma helps to really achieve every person professional excellence in every area of human endeavour. That is why, the political right of centre ideology in India, based on Sanatana Dharma will be able to contribute and inspire the whole nation much better than any of the later day philosophies of pure economic or self-interest-based ideologies. In other words, Sanatana Dharma can be the basis of a modern forward looking true democratic Republic.

# 4

# Political Right

## ARTICULATION OF INDIAN POLITICAL RIGHT: MODI GOVERNMENT'S MISSION

Modi government represents the first major tectonic shift from the Left to the Right in India's political governing philosophy. Thanks to Jawaharlal Nehru's attraction to Fabian Socialism, from 1947 to 2014 the broad political ideology of Indian politics was the left, socialism and communism.

Narendra Modi hailing from the RSS represents the complete antithesis of the leftist ideology. It is this ideological shift that has raised a widespread ongoing debate in the print and electronic media. One example of this is the Op Ed article in *The Hindu* dated September 9, 2015 by G Sampath under the title 'Caste and the Battle for Secularism'. He begins with a question: Is Hindu nationalism a viable project?

> "This is not an idle question.... According to the Constitution, India can never be a 'Hindu nation'. As a nation-state, it must remain politically de-linked from any

> religion. The same question can also be formulated differently: is a secular Indian nationalism a viable project? The answer, according to the publications of the Gita Press, is a resounding 'no'. Their ideology is Hindu nationalism."

The division between the political left and the political right, in every country spans a wide spectrum including economics, sociology, religion, ethical and spiritual values in terms of policy and approach. So far as the economic dimension is concerned, leftists opt for the State controlling the commanding heights of the economy. Communism and socialism or even socialistic pattern of society which Nehru our first Prime Minister advocated, spring from this. Those on the political right believe in liberal, market-led competition to resolve economic issues.

On the sociological side the leftists support the welfare society. The Congress after having lost power after so many years is vigorously championing the welfare state concept using words like inclusive growth and social justice. The Modi government represents in addition to the aspect of inclusive growth, the need for attracting massive investment, improved infrastructure and economic growth which will translate into an explosion of job opportunities. The Prime Minister has been highlighting the advantage of India arising from 3 Ds – Democracy, Demand and Demography. His vigorous tours abroad have had a visible and dramatic impact in attracting the attention of global investors.

The third dimension is religion, ethics and values and it is here that the political right is articulating its vision under the Modi government. Leftists are looking at this issue purely from the religious point of view and are labelling it as an attempt to usher a Hindu nation or a project for Hindu nationalism. G Sampath's article is one more example. This is the blind spot in the leftist intellectual perception.

Who knows? It could be even a case of a hidden agenda of the leftists and those who have thrived on the slogans of poverty elimination and caste- and identity-based vote bank politics! Let us not forget what is happening in Bihar where branding BJP as communal is the rallying cry of the Janata parivar.

The skewed and negative impact of leftist thinking on nurturing ethical values and even patriotism has been highlighted by the detailed and systematic research done by thinkers like Arun Shourie and others like Balbir Punj. In his book *Eminent Historians*, Shourie has brought out how the leftist twist given to history by these historians patronised by the government from 1947, has under-played if not sidelined our 5,000 year old heritage of Sanatana Dharma as the basis of organising governance based on the concept of Dharma. Our values of global vision articulated in the Vedas and the Upanishads. Recalled by Arun Jaitley, the Finance Minister, drew attention to the ancient vision of *'sarve jana sukhino bhavantu'* and *'vasudhaiva kutumbakam'* harking back to the past provides also the rationale for nurturing pride and devotion in our nation. The inspiring impact of national spirit articulated in recent times starting with Swami Vivekananda, is an element which the political left has missed. It is the emphasis on this heritage and healthy practices like yoga which the present government has so prominently highlighted that constitute the articulation of the emerging political right. Together, all these elements constitute the Indian political right.

This indeed is a badly needed corrective in the political spectrum of India and no wonder that the current intellectual establishment nurtured for over six decades with State patronage is vigorously expressing its anxieties and trying to bad mouth the entire effort as the ushering of Hindu nationalism.

After all, the current government has also taken oath of office of loyalty to the Constitution. In fact, no political party in India can function unless it accepts respects and observes the principles of our Constitution.

Let us recall one simple fact. Modi government is defining what constitutes the political right under our constitution. Conservatives always oppose new ideas. Our establishment has intellectuals in every sector. Be it politics academy, culture arts and sociology or whatever are reacting as expected, when a new ideology is defined and emerging. They are out of their comfort zone. Their claims of being rational, modern and secular need to be re-examined in the light of cold reason and current facts.

## ARE WE LOSING OUR NATIONAL IDENTITY?

A series of developments in recent times involving our relations with other nations has raised in me a doubt whether we are losing our identity as a nation called India or Bharat.

The incident involving the Italian marines who shot down two of our fishermen raised a whole set of interesting questions about the criminal aspects of the case, the Vienna Convention and diplomatic immunity, the issue of prosecution in India of foreigners and their undergoing the punishment of imprisonment in their own countries.

After a series of headline grabbing news items for more than a month appealing to the emotions of patriotism and national self-respect, it appears the whole issue has been given a quiet burial.

Another hard emotional issue especially in Tamil Nadu is the issue of the reckless killing of Sri Lankan Tamils in the last phase of the Sri Lankan war against the LTTE in 2009. When heard last the powerful slogan being raised in Tamil Nadu is that the Government of India will have to choose between Tamil Nadu and Sri Lanka as if Tamil Nadu is not part of India.

Yet another incident involving the sensitive subject of India's self-respect as a nation took place in Maldives when the then President was ousted in a surprise development and arrested later on.

The way the West Bengal government led by the Chief Minister Mamata Banerjee bunged a spanner in the discussions of India with Bangladesh on the long standing issue of the waters of the Teesta river raised the issue whether the States in our country are dictating national foreign policy.

In the ultimate analysis, it all boils down to one question – are we losing our identity as a nation called India after more than six decades of Independence? Have the excessive emphasis on regional, caste, language and ethnic identities in our domestic politics steadily eroded the national identity forged and cemented during the heat of our Independence movement against the British rule?

Just compare us with the United States of America. After 9/11 the US government led by President George W Bush felt that American national pride as a super power had been challenged and dented by Al-Qaida dramatically by the destruction of the Twin Towers. Bush resolved to hunt down Osama bin Laden and eliminate the threat of terrorism. In fact he launched the 'war against terror'. Even after a change of leadership and the replacement of the Republican President Bush by the Democratic President Barack Obama, the national strategic goal remains the same. Osama bin Laden was finally hunted down and killed under his watch. No one believes that Al-Qaida has been destroyed. After all, a curious logic of an asymmetry in power drives terrorism. No single individual can be the sole repository of the power of terror. Nevertheless the killing of Osama bin Laden was a huge symbolic gesture soothing three hurt national pride of the United States.

Did we ever display such a sense of national pride and self-respect in any of the issues of foreign policy in recent times mentioned earlier? After all self-respect and pride comes from a sense of national identity. Do we have that vital ingredient which must be the basis of our policy, be it strategic cultural trade or any other sector.

Will we ever develop such a sense of national identity and pride in the context of or inspite of our politics of petty identities based on caste, community, region, language etc?

## BLIND SPOT OF 'SECULARISTS'

I write this in the middle of April 2014 when the fifth phase of the 9 phase general elections is going on. A red hot debate is going on about the possible threat to India's tradition of unity in diversity if a Modi government comes to power.

A typical example of the mindset which reveals the blind spot of the secularist intellectuals is the following extract from the op-ed article in *The Hindu* dated 16th April 2014, titled 'A Modern Day Enlightenment' by Ananya Vajpeyi:

> "If the 2014 general election produces a national government led by the Hindu Right, then what kind of attitudes toward caste can we expect will re-enter the public imagination through the backdoor, if not explicitly and programmatically? Given that Hindutva is founded on a hatred of Gandhi, a dislike of all Gandhian values, and literally, the assassination of the person of Gandhi together with all that he stood for, will we see a glorification of *caturvarnya*, greater caste pride, a renewed confidence in the religious legitimacy of caste differentiation, and newer forms of humiliation and exclusion inflicted upon Dalits?"

The fears expressed above, in my view, are unwarranted. Just look at the following immediate and obvious points.

1. The universal adult suffrage guaranteed by our Constitution is a solid instrument which will ensure that the fears expressed by Ananya Vajpeyi will never become a reality. In fact, there were extensive and vigorous debates in the Constituent Assembly, when this article was included, both pro and anti. At the end of this, our leaders took an instinctive hopeful leap into introducing universal adult suffrage based on their uncanny understanding of the long cultural and spiritual tradition of our country. Our culture which is at least five thousand years old is derived from the Vedas is called the Sanatana Dharma. It looks at the whole world as a family our forefathers

have always believed in allowing free debates on every issue and keeping our minds open for all noble ideas. *Vasudhaiva Kutumbakam* articulates the first concept. The ancient Rigvedic verse (shloka) – *aano bhadra kritavo yantu vishwatah* – denotes the second concept.

2. The very emergence of Narendra Modi hailing from practically the bottom of the social pyramid to become the front-runner for the post of the Prime Minister in the current election is the result of an imaginative insightful and well-executed strategy knitting together voters from the wide spectrum of classes and castes in our country.
3. As we have a parliamentary system modelled on Britain, every policy is the result of debate and extensive discussion to ensure that there is an overall consensus behind it. This automatically ensures that there is not likely to be any extreme distortions causing social disorder or tension in the society.

In the context of these strong factors, we can be sure that the extreme changes as feared by the intellectuals may never become a reality. Let us not forget the comment of VP Singh, the quiet follower of Indira Gandhi, who led the revolt against Rajiv Gandhi in 1984: "Politics is the art of managing contradictions."

## FPP: THE REAL VILLAIN AGAINST BJP

FPP is the short hand for our system of elections under the Representation of Peoples Act. FPP stands for First Past the Post.

This has turned out to be the real villain against the BJP after the general elections of 2014 when ironically this was the very system that propelled BJP to get an incredible majority in the Lok Sabha. Its percentage of votes polled was only around 30% but still it romped home with a stunning majority.

There are honest, competent, public service minded people in every political party in our country today. Thanks to the vicious impact of the FPP when it comes to fighting elections the hard headed party managers consider winnability as the only criterion to distribute tickets to candidates. Almost all of them are compelled to compromise on their principles and ideologies and give tickets to criminals and anti-social elements.

If you want a proof, just recall the recent experience of the BJP in Karnataka when it denied a ticket to BS Yeddyurappa. In the recent Bihar elections, RK Singh (retd IAS), bitterly complained that in his own constituency criminals facing serious charges of crime and anti-social elements were given tickets by BJP. It is ironical that RK Singh, a member of the IAS Bihar cadre was the one who as District Magistrate stopped the Rath Yatra of LK Advani in the 1990s. He retired as the Home Secretary in the UPA-II government. Apparently he was convinced by the beguiling appeal of the BJP that it was a party with a difference. It was a party which walked its talk and lived up to its ideals of good governance. He joined the BJP soon after his retirement and has been bitterly complaining about the BJP's defeat in Bihar.

A slight twist in the rules under the Representation of Peoples Act will help to exorcise the ghost of FPP from our system. The solution will in no way compromise the principles of the Constitution or any laws relating to elections in our country, either in letter or in spirit.

The defeat of BJP in Delhi in January 2015 and in Bihar in November 2015 must at last make the BJP realise the mischief of the FPP. The party leaders must recall the great insight so pithily recorded in one of the James Bond novels (I think it is Dr No):

> "First time is accident, second time is happen stance, third time is no doubt enemy action."

That enemy is FPP which allows a candidate who does not enjoy a real majority in the total votes polled in a constituency to get elected as a 'representative of the people'. When more than two candidates contest, in any constituency, the winning candidate under FPP needs to get only the maximum number of votes polled in the constituency. This may be much less than 50% of the total votes polled.

This can be replaced easily by opting for a system which prevails in France for the election of the President. If in the election the winning candidate does not get 50%+1 of the votes polled, there is a run off between the top two candidates. The winner in the run off election becomes the President. It is this system which General Charles de Gaulle introduced in the 5th Republic after the bitter experience of the revolving door governments of the 4th Republic. The system has been working very smoothly giving stability to French politics.

Thanks to the electronic voting machines, at a small additional cost of say 10%, the Election Commission can adopt a similar system in place of the FPP which has been practised for more than 6 decades. In my view the Election

Commission itself can take the initiative and amend the rules. Unfortunately the Chief Election Commissioner and the members of the Election Commission in recent times with whom I explored this idea seem extremely reluctant to take the initiative.

TN Seshan was the unique Chief Election Commissioner who left his stamp by pushing the envelope of his powers under the Constitution. Every case was tested by the Supreme Court when the matter was brought to the notice of the apex court. Seshan had his way in many matters and established the unique reputation of the Election Commission of India as the most effective and competent commission of a democracy in the world.

We need not lose hope. The government which enjoys a majority in the Lok Sabha in consultation with the Election Commission can introduce the required amendment in the rules of the Representation of the Peoples Act to shift from the FPP to the French style run off system.

If the BJP and the NDA at least learn this lesson from the Delhi and Bihar elections of 2015 and ACT IMMEDIATELY it would be an excellent case of a crisis becoming an opportunity for good governance.

## MODI ONE YEAR ON

Bihar Assembly election was the main subject of all the media in October 2015. As I wrote in mid-October 2015 the topic of the day was beef and a suspected beef eater being killed in Dadri in Uttar Pradesh. Has development ceased to be an election issue in Bihar?

I came across an article in this context – 'Modi One Year On', which refers to an American think-tank called Hudson Institute which has given its assessment of Modi government after completing one year. It says,

> "During the 2014 general election campaign, Modi supporters argued that as an outsider in Delhi, the prime minister would cut India's penchant for bureaucratic red tape. In its first year, the Modi government failed to live up to that expectation. Instead it appears to rely heavily on the bureaucracy for policy guidance, rather than demanding that civil servants put the political leaders' ideas into effect. The BJP-led government was voted into power by a new generation of Indians. The new Indian electorate is aspirational and demands instant gratification and immediate results. Modi's other backer, domestic and foreign business is also impatient for positive results. Markets run on sentiments and until now the upswing in Indian economic growth has been primarily because the markets remain hopeful of change for the better. Prime Minister Modi must act fast before this hopefulness dissipates."

This is representative of the tone and attitude of the observers who look at the NDA government in office at the Centre. Is this assessment correct? Is there some aspect that is missing?

As an old civil servant my take is that this account does not appreciate the realities of the internal dynamics of the Indian political system that has evolved since Independence.

It is true that we inherited the British model for governance with the permanent civil service. But over the years the Indian system of governance has developed its own strengths and weaknesses. The strengths like handling the unprecedented bloodshed of the Partition, meeting the challenge of more than 10 million refugees from East Pakistan in 1970, repeatedly handling the challenges of natural and man made disasters like floods, famines and Bhopal gas leak in 1984 are not considered as achievements at all. Even the three great revolutions – the Green Revolution, the White (Milk) Revolution and the Blue (Space and Nuclear Energy) Revolution – are taken for granted. It is only the failures of the bureaucracy corruption red tape associated with it that are constantly highlighted. This distortion is also reflected in the assessment of the Hudson Institute.

For a badly needed corrective just consider the following:

1. Although ideally political leadership frames the policy its execution on the ground has to be only through the bureaucracy. No leader however competent he may be can by himself do the work of execution in a country like ours of subcontinental dimensions. I had a boss who used to say that a bad master is one who keeps a dog and does the barking himself. Does that mean that the Government has become totally dependent on the bureaucracy?
2. Modi and his team are very clear about their objectives and fundamental ideology. They are certainly not looking to the bureaucracy for policy guidance. They are right of the centre and rooted in the rich and deep Indian heritage and culture. In fact, the main achievement of Modi government is the great tectonic change they have brought in the philosophy and ideology of governance.

From 1947 it has been left of centre. The established intelligentsia is shocked and is still in a state of denial. They are yet to realise that the patronage of the State they enjoyed all these years may no longer be automatic and a given.

3. Apart from this Modi has come to this office with a track record as Chief Minister of Gujarat for 13 years when single-handedly he had to face the hostile machinations of the Central Government which tried every trick in the political trade possible to somehow trap him legally and thereby eliminate him from contesting the elections at all.
4. In this cabinet there are a set of highly competent, committed ministers who are result-oriented and who have also their own track record of achievement. Names like Arun Jaitley, Nitin Gadkari, Manohar Parrikar, Suresh Prabhu, Venkaiah Naidu, Ravi Shankar Prasad, Piyush Goel, come readily to mind.
5. In the last one year foundations have been laid by the Modi government, from where the economy can be given a boost even without big ticket headlines grabbing actions like passing legislation on land acquisition for infrastructure projects. These are areas where the initiative can also be taken by the States and competitive federalism becomes meaningful.
6. Equally important are labour legislation where again some States like Rajasthan have already taken the lead.
7. That is not all. One of the earliest U-turns made by Narendra Modi was in embracing Aadhaar after appreciating its potential for avoiding duplication and

reducing corruption and malpractices. Even though the Supreme Court may not have approved making Aadhaar Card mandatory, there is nothing to prevent heads of institutions like banks, other financial institutions and others who play a role in the economy to voluntarily adopt the Aadhaar Card as a part of KYC system. What can hold them back except their lack of initiative?

In short the economy at the end of one year of Modi government has created enough potential to get out of the trap of policy paralysis of the previous government which it inherited. The best course therefore would be for all players in the economy and governance to take a positive and activist approach instead of being armchair critics.

Let us not also forget that the Achilles heel of the Modi government is the hangover of Congress dominance in the Rajya Sabha and the hostile stand taken by it. Politics remains as the art of the possible.

## UNIFICATION OF INDIA AS A NATION: THE NEXT PHASE

The historic success of the BJP in 2014 general elections has not only brought a regime change but also marks a very significant phase in the emergence of India as a culturally, emotionally and economically integrated modern nation.

BJP fought the election projecting Narendra Modi as their candidate for PM. While other parties particularly the INC (Indian National Congress) stuck to its long-term, time tested-mantra of secularism, Modi presented a clear and vigorous alternative. While Congress's secularism was in practice anti-

Hindu, Modi appealed to the more ideal alternative of a united Indian nation where all citizens including the Hindus have the same right as guaranteed under Article 14 of the Constitution – equality before law and equal protection of the law.

The height of the brazen partiality in favour of the religious minorities was the follow up action taken by the UPA on the basis of Justice Sachar's minority report. The distortions in governance and its hostile impact on Hindus have been highlighted clearly in *The Majority Report* by two retired IPS officers – Ram Kumar Ohri and Jai Prakash Sharma.

They point out on page 2 of their book:

> "Our research has confirmed that it is the Hindus, not the Muslims, who are the most disadvantaged religious group in India. The five major globally recognized economic development indicators are enumerated below:
>
> 1. Infant Mortality
> 2. Child Mortality
> 3. Life Expectancy at Birth
> 4. Degree of Urbanization
> 5. Literacy
>
> By using the convoluted findings of Sachar Committee a policy programme of accelerated discrimination against the majority religious group, the Hindus, was launched by the Prime Minister in June 2006, in the garb of Prime Minister's New 15-Points Programme for Welfare of Minorities."

Good governance was the second major issue of the vigorous and focused campaign conducted by the BJP under the leadership of Narendra Modi. The message was clear that integrity in public life will be a major area of focus and the corrupt will be brought to book. Combined with the impact of the Civil Society campaign launched by Anna Hazare, brought about a major mind shift and a national consensus about reducing corruption which is vital for good governance.

The third item of BJP's campaign led by Modi was getting the economy moving again by ending the policy paralysis of the UPA government.

The first budget introduced by the NDA government sends the right signals of emphasizing the importance of infrastructure development which is vital for economic progress. Inspite of the extremely short time of 2 months the NDA government has brought a change in the national sentiment that better days are ahead. The track record of Narendra Modi in Gujarat for 13 years gives a confidence that India will be entering the next phase of national unification with its roots in our tradition of Sanatana Dharma promoting cultural integration riding on vigorous economic progress.

The ideological opponents of the BJP like Ananya Vajpeyi, author of *Righteous Republic – The Political Foundations of Modern India* (in an article 'Hind Swaraj vs Hindu Rashtra') have cautioned against a face-off between the majoritarians and egalitarians, between the Sangh Parivar and the secular liberal parties, but in the context of the approach articulated by Narendra Modi in his campaign, it is obvious that while the inspiration may come from Hinduism, what will emerge finally is a strong and modern nation rooted in the best values of our tradition.

## WHY IS POLITICAL CORRECTNESS WRONG?

The recent monsoon session of Parliament was washed out, thanks to the Coalgate. This development nevertheless highlighted many negative aspects of India's vigorous democracy. One of them is the key role of political correctness.

What is political correctness? The very name is self-explanatory. It is any stand strategy or policy which is attractive to the people especially the majority, sounds fair and apparently looks ethical and just. It creates a catch 22 situation for those who oppose it.

One of the intriguing realities of Indian politics is that politically correct stands and policies can prove to be horribly incorrect and wrong so far as the larger public interest or national prosperity is concerned.

In the last three days of the monsoon session, the UPA-II government tried to corner the BJP by a PC googly. This was the introduction of super PC bill for reservation quota for SC/ST. It was scuttled by the champions of the OBCs SP who invoked the equally powerful PC mantra of quota within the quota.

PC maxims have been the driving force of Indian politics especially after caste- and identity-based politics emerged thanks to the decline of national parties and growth of regional parties.

At the end of the NDA regime when the government projected its achievements by the slogan of 'India Shining' the Congress invented a PC slogan focusing on the 'aam admi'. India may be shining for some in the post-1991 economic liberalization period but not for the aam aadmi for whom India was still dark. The politically correct approach for policy formulation was to focus on the people below poverty line (BPL) and make some of their basic needs like food, education, health and employment as rights. NREGA now renamed as MGNREGA was the first programme based on this PC maxim.

The second focused on education resulting in the Right to Education Act. The third was focused on food. The legislation for food security has been for the moment derailed thanks to the serious doubts about the availability of adequate food grains by the concerned ministries.

NREGA has been implemented with mixed results. NREGA has had a negative impact so far as the availability of agricultural labour is concerned. This has rendered the already strained agriculture into a non-viable activity.

One combined impact of all these politically correct policies is the development of a culture of entitlement among the BPL population. The message has gone that one need not make any effort to meet one's needs. The generosity of the welfare state is available to anyone BPL. This culture of entitlement has resulted in the vast majority of people developing what I would call the *'langar'* (freeloader) mentality.

Another negative impact of the langar mentality is the erosion of the work ethic.

Creation of wealth is impossible without this.

This erosion of the work ethic has seriously damaged the country realizing its full potential for wealth creation and prosperity. No wonder the much hyped India story is developing a shade of grey.

The long-term consequences of the erosion of the work ethic can be seen in the paradox of two States – Kerala and West Bengal – which have long been under leftist or left leaning governments.... The population of these States is bright, hard-working and Kerala has long been a leader in literacy and human development index. Nevertheless inspite of the tremendous efforts made by the State governments, it has been very difficult to attract investment, trigger economic growth and wealth generation.

A classic example is an anecdote relating to Dr Verghese Kurien, the miracle man of the White Revolution. It appears that once Ms Gowri Amma, Industries Minister of Kerala, came to Anand in Gujarat, headquarters of Amul/National Dairy Development Board (NDDB) and was duly impressed by the progress achieved. She rushed into the room of Dr Kurien and asked him, "Dr Kurien, you are from Kerala. You have come out of the State and achieved so much? Why did you not do anything in Kerala itself?"

Dr Kurien deadpanned, "The problem in Kerala is that there are too many Malayalis!" I have confirmed this story from Dr Kurien himself.

So we come back to the basic question. Is political correctness wrong when it comes to wealth creation and economic development?

## FROM FATHER INDIA TO MOTHER INDIA

Smriti Irani, the articulate TV actor-turned Vice President of the BJP, came with the most insightful comment on the tectonic political change that the 2014 general elections have brought. The essence of what Irani said in a TV debate was this:

> "The RSS is accused of having the remote control over the BJP government." After all, BJP is a part of the Sangh Parivar. Other political parties are dominated by families of individual leaders. The Nehru-Gandhi family dominates the INC, Mulayam Singh Yadav's family dominates the Samajwadi Party; Mayawati dominates Bahujan Samaj Party; the Karunanidhi family is Dravida Munnetra Kazhagam (DMK) and so on.
>
> "There is a fundamental difference between those parties and the BJP. The relationship in the other political parties, between the leader and the party cadres, is that of a master-slave. In the case of RSS and BJP, it is a relationship between a mother and her child."

It is hence that Narendra Modi, the Prime Minister designate, broke down when Advani used the word *'kripa'* (grace), that Modi had showed towards BJP. Modi continued his speech by referring to the fact, "for me just as Bharatmata is my mother, the BJP is also another mother. A son can only do service to the mother, how can he shower grace on her?"

### Equality for All, but More Equality for Minorities!

In short, Modi represents, in sharp relief, the difference between two types of Indians. Those who are traditional and thinking in the native idiom about the country and for whom it is Mother India; and those who look at India through western eyes and for whom it is Father India. This perception of India through western eyes brings the outsider's perspective. This is at the root of the secularism and pseudo secularism debate. Modi has defined secularism to mean that all are Indians and religion, language and ethnic differences do not matter. On the other hand, for the English educated, western-minded intelligentsia, secularism means ensuring that the religious minorities are specially protected by way of reservation, quotas, even violating Article 14 of the constitution, offering special programmes and concessions. To quote the famous line from George Orwell's *Animal Farm* – for them "All Indians are equal, but the minorities are more equal than others."

Narendra Modi was subjected to single-minded hostility and 24 × 7 scrutinies for the last 12 years. The UPA government and the whole bag of dirty tricks to somehow trap him into a criminal case so that he cannot contest the elections, failed dramatically. Modi has brought about a tectonic change in Indian politics. This is because his critics missed the following points, which were the ground realities:

## Gujarat Growth

The villagers in Uttar Pradesh, Bihar and the east where the BJP was practically invisible if not non-existent, were influenced by the tales about peace, prosperity and the job opportunities available in Gujarat under Modi's rule inspite of the demonisation by the media and caste-based parties of the Hindu belt. Even in distant Assam, West Bengal and Nagaland, this basic reality persuaded the voters to vote for Modi. No wonder in Assam it was not the Gogoi wave but the Modi wave that prevailed administering a shock to Tarun Gogoi who found to his dismay, 10 out of the 11 constituencies in Assam had voted for Modi.

## Vibrancy Unrestricted

Narendra Modi represents the best elements of the Gujarati entrepreneurial spirit and has created an industry-friendly, entrepreneur-friendly, wealth and job-creating environment. It is not only Adani and Ambani but also very large number of entrepreneurs, right across the industrial spectrum that has created the vibrant Gujarat.

Above all Modi represents the true spirit of the Sanatana Dharma, which makes an excellent synthesis between eternal values like treating the whole world as a family (*vasudhaiva kutumbakam*) and also keeping an open mind that welcomes change and all noble ideas. As the Rigveda says – *aano bhadra kritavo yantu vishwatah* (let the noble thoughts come to me from all directions).

## Success of SCAM

A Hindu does not mean he is backward looking and only taking pride in the achievements of the past. He is the one who keeps an open mind and welcomes the latest technological development. It is, therefore, not surprising that after the results it is recognised that this election was dominated by the information technology or to put it lightly, SCAMs – Social media, Clouds, Analytics and Mobility – which are the basic pillars of modern information technology. Modi's campaign exploited SCAM in all senses with deadly effect!

Mother India has replaced Father India. We can therefore, look for a bright future irrespective of the caste or religion to which we belong. The Niagara of advice that the secular intelligentsia is flooding Modi with, is therefore, thoroughly unnecessary.

## MODI AND THE REINVENTION OF RSS

Ever since the Modi government took office in May 2014, the establishment intelligentsia which has had free and unchallenged run of practically the entire spectrum of political, academic and social institutions has been in a state of shock. They are in a mood of denial and practically every action of the Modi government is being viewed with a hostile microscope. In the process, some of the major policy directions and the ideological evolution which the BJP and its basic inspiration, the RSS are undergoing are lost sight of.

One example of the establishment intelligentsia's secular perception about the Modi government and especially the RSS, is an article by G Sampath in *The Hindu* dated 16th February 2016 in connection with the current debate about nationalism arising out of the turmoil in the central universities like Jawaharlal Nehru University, University of Hyderabad and earlier in IIT (Madras). In the course of his article Sampath makes the following comments:

> "Already, according to the national taxonomy of the Sangh Parivar, Adivasis in central India, Dalit students, Left intellectuals, human rights activists, a certain religious minority, anti-nuclear activists, beef eaters, non-haters of Pakistan, inter-religious couples, homosexuals, and labour activists are anti-nationals. If we take into account Monday's episode of goonda nationalism at Patiala House in New Delhi, we must expand the list to include journalists, people dressed like JNU students, anyone without an identity card, anyone recording goonda nationalists in action, and anyone opposed to the said goonda nationalists.

At this rate, it seems likely that by the time the National Democratic Alliance (NDA) finishes its term, the vast majority of Indians would have turned into anti-nationals. The only cure for their anti-nationalism being the healing nationalist brutality of an Akhil Bharatiya Vidyarthi Parishad (ABVP) or Bajrang Dal lynch mob, while India's nationalist police presides over the ceremony, peacefully.

What exactly is goonda nationalism? A goonda nationalist is anyone who arrogates to himself the job of certifying citizens as anti-national.

He goes on to elaborate,

"Goonda nationalism is not a new phenomenon. The German historian Arthur Rosenberg, in his book *Fascism as a Mass Movement* refers to two conditions as prefiguring in the rise of fascism; the rise of right-wing nationalism, and an active connivance between the State and identitarian storm troopers. What India has witnessed over the past month, first in Hyderabad Central University (HCU) and now in Jawaharlal Nehru University (JNU), is early consolidation of these two conditions for the furtherance of an agenda that we shall not call fascist because, as we've been assured repeatedly by eminent Indian liberals, India is too diverse and Indian democracy too resilient for us to use the f-word."

"India's bane has been the failure of its self-proclaimed 'constitutional' liberals to acknowledge that the forces of Hindutva and economic liberalism (or neo-liberalism) are a package deal."

> "In their heated embrace of economic liberalism, India's liberal elites looked away as the State either went after or neglected the interests of labourers, the urban poor, the farmers, the landless, the land-poor – the vast majority of whom are from socially marginalized castes. Now they find the State looking away as their own liberal freedoms come under siege by State-endorsed illiberal forces."

I am afraid I cannot agree. Has RSS remained frozen in time and is totally unaware or insensitive to the drastic changes that have taken place in the last 80 years since it was founded?

The organizing of the Shakhas where the members of the Sangh wear khakhi shorts (now brown trousers) and carry out exercises may be reminiscent of the Hitler youth. But the RSS has not remained frozen in time or ideology.

It is surprising that the secular and establishment intelligentsia who consider themselves to be modern and progressive in their thinking and are aware of the developments in the world, somehow assume that organizations other than theirs will remain frozen in time and may not change at all.

An intimate insider's glimpse of what has been happening in RSS itself can be had from a very perceptive book *Lost Years of the RSS* written by Sanjiv Kelkar. Kelkar who has been closely associated with the movement and he gives an insider's perception of the various currents of thoughts and leadership styles of the different Sarsanghchalaks who have led the RSS in the last eighty years.

The initial idea of Dr Hedgewar who founded the RSS on Vijayadashami day in 1925 was only to unite the Hindu community to which majority of the people for our country belongs. But the subsequent development of the RSS under his successor Guruji Golwalkar brought a different approach. Balasaheb Deoras brought further changes.

Nevertheless, this much has been consistent stream of thought through the RSS and re-elected in its track record. The basic inspiration comes from Swami Vivekananda and the consciousness/realization that majority of us in this country are inheritors of the Sanatana Dharma which is popularly called Hinduism.

In fact the word Hindu itself is the name given to our religion by the foreigners who could not appreciate the nuances and special aspects of our religion.

As mentioned earlier, the immediate inspiration for the RSS came from Swami Vivekananda. Swami Vivekananda himself was the product of late 19th century social, political and religious renaissance especially in Bengal of the Indian and Hindu national consciousness thanks to the impact of the British rule.

There have been two streams of spiritual tradition in our country. One has been the true spiritual quest at the individual level represented by seers like Ramakrishna Paramahamsa, Aurobindo and Ramana Maharshi. The other are reformers who came on scene from time to time and tried to bring about changes in the way of life of Hindus by emphasizing the basic values which constitute the essence of Sanatana Dharma. It is the combined efforts of these two streams that kept our tradition of Hinduism going and this country united as a unique example of unity in diversity, a multi-lingual multi-ethnic multi-cultural wonder. The RSS when it started was inspired by this tradition.

Although the focus of the RSS to begin with was only on holding back to the basic values and culture of the country, as an organization, it could not be indifferent to other aspects of life like politics and governance. That is why the shaping of the organization also was inspired by the parallel development in other fields.

In his book *Lost Years of the RSS*, Kelkar points out how, while the RSS was initially focused only on the concept of Swadeshi, it could not be indifferent to the major international developments like the globalization of the economy and the modern world which is borderless but which is united on the basis of competition and at the same time with the emphasis on ethics in business.

Surprisingly, the collapse of ideologies like Communism has once again created an opportunity for refocusing on the need for ethical element in business. And, it is here that the RSS and BJP with their focus on our cultural roots in Sanatana Dharma have an advantage and a long-term inherent robustness over all others opposed to it to deliver good governance of the country.

The Modi government represents the first totally and authentic home-grown ideology for ethical or Dharmic good governance operating on the inclusive principle of *sarve jana sukhino bhavantu*.

The voters of India have decisively rejected the Left of centre secular ideology that was followed by all post-independent governments since 1947. They have given an opportunity for a genuine Right of Central Government.

What we are witnessing is the reinventing and reshaping of the organizations of both RSS and BJP in the light of the basic principles of Sanatana Dharma. Narendra Modi heading the government and Mohan Bhagwat heading the RSS have found a common frequency of articulating an ideology of the Right of the central government, tailor-made for our own Indian requirement. They are also laying a firm foundation by harking back to the fundamentals of Sanatana Dharma which have a very close resonance for good governance.

The vision of *vasudhaiva kutumbakam* is an inclusive one. So is the Upanishadic dictum of "*sarve bhavantu sukhinah, sarve santu niramayah, sarve bhadrani pashyantu, ma kashchit duhkha bhagbhavet*".

It is this important shift that is taking place which is missed by the current commentators who form the vast majority of the boisterous establishment and 'secular' intelligentsia today.

That is why G Sampath is wrong when he says, "India's bane has been the failure of its self-proclaimed liberals to acknowledge that the forces of Hindutva and economic liberalism (or neo-liberalism) are a package deal."

# 5

# Good Governance

## CREATING 21ST CENTURY AMULS: ETI, THE NEXT BIG IDEA

Dr Verghese Kurien was one of the most effective builders of 20th century India. The White Revolution, leading to India emerging as the biggest producer of milk in the world was thanks to his vigour, vision and a powerful idea fully backed by unstinted government policy support. The co-operative model which protected the interests of the producers covering millions of rural farmers and especially women was Dr Kurien's unique achievement. He was successful in realizing his vision because the government provided a vital policy protection by banning any competition from the private sector so far as milk was concerned.

The idea of protecting the co-operatives from competition could work in the 20th century when the State played a key role in the economy. The 21st century's model of economic development is based on globalized liberal open market economies. The role of the government is to ensure a level playing field in the market and protection for any sector is anathema.

## In this Changed Context is it Possible to Build New Versions of Amul?

The quintessence of Amul was to ensure that the interests of the large number of the poor producers were fully safeguarded and they shared totally in the prosperity that came out of the enterprise. The net result was thousands of the poor agricultural families found that their standard and quality of life improved solidly over the years. This was indeed unique in our country with a tradition of more than 5,000 years.

Self-Help Groups (SHGs) emerged as the successor. These self-help groups mostly of women and the poor, were the result of the efforts of another visionary in Bangladesh Dr Muhammad Yunus, who was honoured with a Nobel Peace Prize.

Micro-financing was propagated as an ideal solution to spread prosperity without straining the resources of the State. Unfortunately in recent times, this model has come into disrepute as an instrument for unscrupulous conmen to exploit the banking system and the poor.

Public-private partnership (PPP) was touted as the next option to combine the benefits of large infrastructure projects with public benefit without allowing the private sector to exploit monopoly positions. Unfortunately this model in our country appears to have lost its credibility at the moment, thanks to the series of scams which have grabbed the attention of the media like the 2G and Coalgate.

In this context a quiet pragmatic solution being worked out appears to herald the next big idea. Fortunately this has a multi-dimensional impact and potential covering culture, tradition, public safety and public health.

A great part of our cultural tradition is linked with rivers and the holy places on the banks of the rivers. Ganga is the most prominent example of a river symbolizing the history, culture and tradition of a nation. Jawaharlal Nehru in his book *Discovery of India* became poetic in describing the river and the rich tradition it represents.

Unfortunately the river Ganga which has been worshipped as a sacred river with not only the religious significance of washing away one's sins but also medically claimed for having healing powers, has in recent times lost its claim for purity. In many places along its more than 1,000 km plus journey to the sea the river has become highly polluted. The degree of pollution varies from place to place. It is particularly bad around holy cities which attract millions of pilgrims. Many major cities have come up along the route and quite a few of them have large industries employing millions of people. The effluents of these factories also flow into the Ganga apart from the sewage of the cities which are not always fully treated.

The number of dams and barrages along the river has had a negative impact especially near the holy cities.

Thanks to the vision and initiative of Rajiv Gandhi, the Government of India launched in 1980s a major initiative for cleaning the river Ganga and tributaries like Yamuna, Kosi etc. Unfortunately, though thousands of crores of rupees have been spent so far there has not been much progress. The condition of the river Yamuna in holy places like Mathura and Vrindavan has become critical. Except for the monsoon season when the river has better flow thanks to the floods, what flows in Yamuna during the rest of the time is the sewage water of upstream cities like Delhi. This is particularly emerging as a sensitive issue so far as the pilgrims are concerned who come to the holy places on the river bank specially with the objective bathing in the river. The obvious solution to the problem is to ensure that a sewage treatment plant is installed near the holy places before the water is allowed from upstream cities. This calls for heavy investment and somehow in implementing the plan so far, adequate sewage treatment plants and their maintenance have not been ensured. It is in finding a solution to this problem that a business model which can successfully replace the Amul model is emerging.

The idea being explored is of forming a company involving all the temples of Mathura and Vrindavan as shareholders. This company in turn can enter into a contract with a venture capital fund which can advance the money upfront for a sewage treatment plant and its regular maintenance. The recovery of the cost of the plant and maintenance can be spread over a loan period of twenty years which will be paid by the company of temple managements.

This in turn appears to be a solution to the problem of ensuring public good of safe bathing water in Yamuna without getting permanently caught in the catch-22 situation of no budget and no investment. It will be interesting to watch the success of this experiment.

What shall we call this post-SHG, post-micro-finance, post-PPP model? The promoters have come up with a new alphabet soup – ETI (Education, Technology and Innovation). All these elements are there all the time in the Amul and the other models. ETI makes this explicit and points out the sequence of operation in the model. After all new problems need new recipes.

## CALLING THE BLUFF OF 'BLACK MONEY FIGHTERS'

Black money is the oxygen for corruption in all sectors of our public life. Corruption is the oxygen for black money.

In recent times the humongous amount of black money estimated to be around 1.4 trillion dollars stashed by Indian citizens and especially the top layers of politics, bureaucracy, business and other professions has dramatically grabbed the attention of all genuine patriots of our country. In fact in the last three years, all the major anti-corruption movements have drawn their inspiration from this revelation.

As usual our politicians have let off a Niagara of words. Our leaders are victims of the MAFA (Mistaking Announcement For Achievement) syndrome. Right from our honourable Prime Minister and the honourable President when he was Finance Minister have waxed eloquent on this issue vowing to bring back all this amount to India. The Prime Minister promised during the 2009 elections, that in hundred days of UPA-II, this will be achieved. The Finance Minister Pranab Mukherjee launched a campaign to track down money and money launderers. A well-publicized effort was made about the vigorous initiative of the Government of India entering into double tax avoidance treaties with nearly hundred countries.

The net result as of today is a big zero.

## Is there a Solution to this Problem?

Fali Nariman, one of the finest legal brains of India has made a suggestion in his capacity as a nominated member of the Rajya Sabha. His suggestion is disarming. It is simplicity in itself.

Government of India has sovereign powers. Subject to the provisions of the Constitution, the government can make laws affecting its citizens. Exercising this power, Nariman suggests that government can enact a law and looking to the urgency, issue an ordinance to the effect that all funds held in tax havens will vest in the Government of India in an authority to be created called the Custodian of Funds of Indian Citizens in tax havens.

It is not a case of the government misusing its sovereign powers to become a sovereign robber. In the case of each citizen who can show to the custodian that the funds in the tax havens were acquired by him lawfully on which he has also paid the tax dues, his funds will be released to him. Those who have got unaccounted and illegally earned wealth will be trapped like a thief at night stung by a scorpion during his attempt to steal. Such people will be forced to keep quiet and the money will all vest in Government of India.

This is a neat solution which does not call for any elaborate administrative arrangement or heavy expenses. As a layman who is no expert in law, I respect the suggestion of Nariman and if the government and the authorities are really interested in fighting corruption they should immediately implement it.

Those who genuinely want to fight black money will readily accept it.

Those who only pretend to be fighting black money will find umpteen excuses for not taking any effective action. It appears that the Government of India is not committed to fight corruption and black money.

The then Finance Minister Pranab Mukherjee explained to the Parliament, that there are a number of difficulties and legal hurdles in bringing back the funds to India. This shows that the Government of India and other political leaders who claim to be fighting the black money menace and money laundering are only enacting a charade. As everyone knows it is possible to wake up a person who is sleeping but not someone who is pretending to be sleeping.

One possible legal challenge would be whether the foreign governments and the banks will honour the Government of India's order. There are precedents internationally like diplomatic immunity to ensure that the law suggested by Fali Nariman can be defended. Recently the Information Technology Act, 2000 has also provided under Section 78, the authority of the Government of India to take actions against Indian citizens who commit cyber crimes which may originate outside India. Yet another law which can further empower the Government of India is the nearly 2 decades old Benami Transactions Prohibition Act 1989 under which Benami properties can be confiscated. This is not yet implemented because the rules have not yet been promulgated, even after two decades, thus making that law into a mockery. By plugging this loop hole the suggestion of Nariman can be smoothly implemented calling the bluff once and for all of all the 'fighters of black money'.

## USHERING ACCOUNTABILITY IN GOVERNANCE

2013 marks the year when the so-called millennium generation of Indians born in 2000 enters its teens. Thirteen is a significant landmark in the life of every individual and generation. It marks the transition from childhood to adolescence.

Sociologists and commentators on current affairs are trying to assess how this generation of Indians is evolving. For example, the spontaneous explosion of collective disgust against the ghastly gang rape in Delhi on 16th December 2012 has been commented upon by Prof Arvind Panagariya in an article titled 'A Tale of Two Tragedies' in *The Times of India* (Chennai), January 12, 2013. He has compared the response of the US government to the massacre of 26 children and other innocents in a school in New Town Connecticut in December 2012 and the gang rape of a 23 year old woman medical student in New Delhi in the same month on 16th as follows:

> (In contrast to the prompt humane and sympathetic response of President Obama downwards the entire set of authorities in the US.) In New Delhi, the aging leadership greeted the news of the gang rape with total indifference. Having deliberately insulated itself for years from the reality that real people with real problems live in the cities too, it went about business as usual. It was a full week of swelling crowds and rising rage of tens of thousands of men and women in the streets that finally led the Prime Minister's Office to break its silence. Even then, the December 23 statement by it reflected aloofness, opening with the words, "We are all joined in our concern for the young woman...." The slight personal touch, with this line

> rephrased as, "My wife, my family and I are all joined in our concern..." came only in the terse televised speech by the Prime Minister the next day.

This social activism of the millennium generation is markedly different from earlier generations like us. In our times the middle class was watching the political developments closely but any criticism about issues like malpractices, corruption, lack of propriety, lack of accountability etc was confined only to the drawing room conversations, letters to the editor in the newspapers and in recent times, television channels. The rare exception was 26/11 – the terrorist attack in Mumbai when the middle class of intellectuals and professionals came out in the streets to hold candle light vigils and demonstrate openly. An earlier example of this type was in 1985 in Gujarat when the middle class demonstrated against the reservation in education for backward classes. Unfortunately the momentum of these demonstrations did not last long. It was soon business as usual.

The demonstration against the recent gang rape shows that this generation of youth may be different. They have the advantage of technology like the internet and the social networks. Communication is now instantaneous. And what is more this generation is willing to walk its talk. The delayed reaction of the prime minister is an example of the political class realizing that this generation cannot be tackled by the tactics adopted in the past.

Does this mean we are likely to witness the ushering of more accountability in government because the current generation will not accept the traditional excuses or will this generation also become mellow with age and lose its fire?

Every generation has displayed in its youth changing values and these have left a lasting mark on governance. The freedom movement itself and the post-Independence developments like the emphasis on the freedom of expression during emergency are two examples. Part of this is directly attributable to technology. The current agitation by the youth would not be possible but for the infrastructure of the internet and the social networking sites. It will be interesting to watch the future developments.

Depending on the momentum of the civil society movements long-term changes are introduced which become game-changers. A recent example is the Right To Information (RTI) Act, 2005. It will no longer be possible for the government to hide behind the Official Secrecy Act.

Thanks to the changes in the post-emergency period President's rule cannot be introduced in a State at the whim of the Central Government. It will be interesting to watch whether the activism of the millennium generation combine with modern communication technology will usher greater accountability in government.

## CVC'S CINDERELLA – VIGEYE (VIGilance EYE)

9th December 2010 was declared by the United Nations as the World Anti-Corruption Day. The CVC as the premier body of the Government of India to fight corruption in the organizations of the Central Government, not only celebrated the day but took a rare initiative to launch a new tool to synergize technology, government and the citizens to fight corruption in government. As a former CVC (September 1998-2002), I was asked to inaugurate the CVC's imaginative initiative which I did very happily.

'VIGEYE' was a program based on software which can be loaded as an application (App) in the mobile phones. With this App any whistleblower or a citizen who wants to expose any case of corruption that has taken place, that is taking place or likely to take place, can do so by SMS to the CVC. He could include details like pictures, documents, voice recordings etc. A member of the CVC (currently R Sri Kumar, IPS, Retd) was to look into the case and take urgent follow up action. The privacy of the whistleblower was guaranteed in the server maintained by the system administrator of VIGEYE. There were built in systems to ensure that the contents could be publicized and corrective action initiated.

During the last three years VIGEYE has helped the CVC particularly to take preventive action to check corruption and also ensure that the guilty are brought to book. Unfortunately, majority of the whistle blowers are from the civil society. The recent campaigns of Anna Hazare and Baba Ramdev have created an unprecedented awareness among the citizens about the massive and all pervasive corruption prevailing in every sphere of our public life and governance today. Unfortunately, a majority of the whistleblowers do not know the limited jurisdiction of the CVC. Hence the complaints received by VIGEYE included individual grievances, corrupt practices in the States and other organizations including the private sector.

The full impact of VIGEYE as an effective tool to forge a public-private partnership in fighting corruption can be realized only if every vigilance organization, be it in the States or the private sector or elsewhere also have a similar system. The CVC software could be appropriately modified and adapted to suit the different organizations. All this requires significant investment in the computer systems and adequate human resources to take follow up action.

Recently on 12th July 2013, at Chennai, a local NGO called 'The Fifth Pillar' invited the Vigilance Commissioner Sri Kumar, to launch VIGEYE in Tamil Nadu. I attended the function.

I was shocked to learn that even though VIGEYE was useful and proved its worth in attracting significant number of responses, it is still languishing. Not a single rupee has been provided for in the budget of the CVC or earmarked for deepening and widening the VIGEYE network.

One can imagine the tremendous impact that a massive expansion of this tool will have if all organizations across the spectrum of government – in the Centre and States, in the private sector, NGOs and others start using it. IT will become the standard first step in fighting corruption and ensure that valid and reliable information about corrupt practices is brought to the notice of those authorities who are expected to take preventive, predictive or corrective (including punitive) action to eradicate this cancer in our body politic.

In these days of all round corruption and scams, with the 24 × 7 media screaming against it, why must VIGEYE languish as the Cinderella of the CVC?

## FROM PARROT TO EAGLE

The CBI (Central Bureau of Investigation) is facing a critical moment in its history thanks to the scrutiny of its functioning by the Supreme Court in the Coalgate case.

Instead of being a free, vigorous, sharp eyed and fast eagle, CBI has been behaving like a caged parrot with many masters, singing in its master's voice. July 10th 2013 will witness the next scene in this unfolding drama when the government will place its decision about ensuring the legal independence of CBI as an agency for investigation.

It is a sad fact, the CBI has today come to symbolize bad and poor governance. The basic function of good governance is the establishment of the rule of law. This means protecting those citizens who observe the law and punishing those who violate it. When any crime is committed there must be a quick, fair and thorough investigation. The evidence must be placed before a court of law which will decide the case after assessing it.

Unfortunately from the early days of our Independence in 1947 the police forces of the State governments have been badly compromised and politicized. Under our Constitution, our country is a union of States. According to the list 2 of the 7th schedule of our Constitution, law and order is a subject under the exclusive jurisdiction of the States. The Central Government had to enact the Delhi Special Police Establishment Act to cover the jurisdiction of the national capital and areas like the land belonging to the Railways. The Delhi Special Police Establishment later on became the CBI. It developed a reputation for professional competence and impartiality thanks to the excellent leadership it had at the level of the early Directors like DP Kohli, FV Arul and others. In fact every IPS officer deems it an honour to be deputed to the CBI. The poor reputation of the State police and the image of the CBI many a time led to the demand for any major crime that took place in any State, to be entrusted to the CBI for investigation. Under the law the CBI cannot investigate any case beyond the direct jurisdiction described in the Delhi Special Police Establishment Act without the concurrence of the State governments.

The CBI investigates two types of cases. The first type is cases of corruption under the Prevention of Corruption Act 1988 and the second is major criminal cases including those which cover more than one State.

The Supreme Court is the apex court of the country and it is the final word when it comes to the interpretation of the law and the Constitution. Thanks to the judgment of Justice JS Verma in the Vineet Narain case, also known as the Havala case, December 1997, the Central Vigilance Commission was identified as the body to supervise the CBI and ensure that no political pressure was brought on it. The selection of the Director as well as practically all senior officers of the CBI is made by a committee headed by the CVC and other members of the Commission, the Secretary Personnel, Secretary Home and Director CBI. It is from the panel of names recommended by this committee that the Department of Personnel which is the administrative ministry for the CBI, issues the appointment orders. The Director CBI is also ensured of a 2 year tenure. He cannot be transferred in between, without the concurrence of the CVC. Unfortunately inspite of this special provision the CBI has apparently been reduced to a tool of the government of the day, being increasingly used for meeting political ends.

Inspite of the sincere effort of the Supreme Court to ensure the independent functioning of the CBI there is one key aspect which they cannot guarantee. In the ultimate analysis it is the character and personality of the people who will occupy the posts in the CBI as an organization that will decide whether it functions independently. The legal framework can only provide restrictions on interference or the brazen misuse of the organization for settling political scores but when it comes to how the officials of the CBI behave, it depends entirely on their values and sense of professionalism. Many a time a crisis is also an opportunity. Let us hope the current crisis of CBI will turn out to be an opportunity thanks to the intervention of the Supreme Court and make it an important instrument for good governance. Let us hope that the parrot will at last learn to become a soaring eagle.

## GOLDEN STANDARD IN PUBLIC LIFE

Information technology (IT) has had a great impact in our everyday life. Thanks to the internet and the explosive revolutions in communication technology, the world has become a global village. Everything is instantaneous. 24 × 7 news channels are all the time after 'breaking news'. Thanks to Facebook and other social networks, everyone is broadcasting his life every moment to the whole world. At the same time the attention span of people has become minimal. No one has the time to pause and think. We are being constantly subjected to 24 × 7 stimulation by one scandal or another.

The UPA-II government has become a great source of this type of continuous scandals. Before you can digest one scam comes another and then another and so on.

A few days back we got a great diversion for a week from all the political scandals. Spot fixing, match fixing, bookies and betting in cricket, the most popular game for us Indians, occupied the electronic media totally. For a change politics took a back seat. There was a suspicion that perhaps even this was a diversionary tactic thought out by corrupt politicians who had fertile imagination. Who knows? The focus on cricket might have been by design.

This raises a natural question. We can understand the public concern in the media on issues relating to corruption and good governance which affect public life but why this focus on sport and betting? After all there are other entertainments like horse racing where betting is accepted. The civil society movements in the last three years, like the Anna Hazare's movement focused on the public life and the need for transparency and integrity in that sector.

A strong leitmotif of ethics pervades all debates on public affairs in our media especially television. The same ethical tone also dominated the debates on cricket match fixing. The question is: Should we apply the same Procrustean standards for sports and public life?

The political class in their defence pointed out that the intellectual middle class sitting in the comfort of their drawing rooms can not theorise and preach in the media on the standards of public life without facing and experiencing the rough and tumble off politics on the ground.

I suggest that we must adopt what I would call the 'golden standard' or the '22 carat standard' when it comes to integrity, cleanliness and transparency in public life.

The 24 carat gold is the purest form of gold and is most valuable when it comes to price. Unfortunately that pure gold is not suitable for making valuable long lasting jewels. It has to be diluted to 22 carat for making them. If we further dilute it to 18 carat which many in the western world use, it has not much value as far as us Indians are concerned. If we want the maximum gold content and also pragmatic use, it has to be 22 carat.

When it comes to public life also we should adopt this pragmatic standard which our women have used by tradition for generations so far as gold jewels are concerned. We cannot expect every public servant to have the 24 carat standard. But certainly we can expect the 22 carat level and not go down further. That is why it makes sense to insist on strict rules and regulations to check corruption and malpractices in public governance but in other fields like sport and entertainment we can frame pragmatic regulations which many other countries have adopted and permit practices like betting with transparent rules that are strictly implemented.

## INCREASE THE SIZE AND DECREASE THE POWER

The Comptroller and Auditor General of India is an important authority under our Constitution. It is entrusted with the function of auditing the financial accounts of the Government of India and all the States and union territories. It reports to the Parliament. Thanks to the series of mega scams from 2010 one after the other, the CAG is very much in the public eye. Not only that, it has also placed the Government of India, especially the UPA-II in politically embarrassing situations.

In October 2012 there were media reports that V Narayanasamy, Minister of State in Prime Minister's office, had indicated that the Government of India was thinking of converting the CAG into a 3-member body like the Election Commission and the CVC. This provoked opposition from

BJP and a vigorous debate in the media. Many senior bureaucrats felt that this move was in reality an attempt to dilute the power of the CAG which from the time of Independence has been a single member body. The Minister of State promptly denied that there was any such move as attributed to him. Nevertheless the fact that such an idea has been mooted by the former CAG VK Shunglu in his report on the CWG scam is still doing the rounds.

Some papers have welcomed the move. The reasons for welcoming the move are the following:

1. The mandate of the CAG to audit the accounts of the union and State governments is quite substantial and is becoming increasingly complex. In this context three heads could be more efficient than one. This will boost transparency in government accounting.
2. The argument that multi-member CAG would dilute efficacy is not acceptable because institutions cannot depend on individual personalities to function optimally. A consultative approach would impart vibrancy in terms of work culture and ideas.

In my view the above arguments are not valid and do not reflect the harsh realities on the ground. The Election Commission was from 1952 till 1984 a single member body but was converted into a multi-member body when the Chief Election Commissioner RVS Peri Shastri, a quiet but firm legal expert objected to the government coming up with populist measures after the election to Parliament were notified.

The single member format was resumed after Peri Shastri left the office. It was revived in 1989 when the formidable

TN Seshan was appointed as CEC. For any impartial observer it was an open display of political muscle power of the government to check the freedom of operation of the CEC by placing him in a position to work for a consensus in day to day operations.

If further proof is needed, I was witness to the government's strategy of increasing the size as a way of reducing the power and flexibility of operations of any authority when I became the first CVC in September 1998 following the judgement in the Supreme Court of the Havala case. The CVC which was a single member body from 1964 to 1998 was converted into a three member body. The tenure of the CVC was also reduced from five years to four years.

One can still make a theoretical justification but the realities are there for all to see. After all when an individual has the power of an office, he can operate more freely than when he is required to operate as a part of a team, where he can be outvoted. I suppose a multi-member body improves transparency because the sources of leakage are more!

*Tailpiece:* Incidentally in the current situation of fractured politics and coalition governments, a Constitutional amendment of any type is a near impossibility unless it is of the type which will get universal support from the members of Parliament like a massive increase in their pay and perquisites!

## IS ANTI-CORRUPTION MOVEMENT ANTI-DEMOCRATIC?

From 2010 our national debate has been dominated by the exposure of corruption scams and two activist movements focused on removal of corruption from public life. Anna Hazare and the activists around him called Team Anna or India Against Corruption, focused their energies on drafting and enacting the Jan Lokpal Bill as the single point solution for corruption in public life. Baba Ramdev focused his movement on bringing back to India the estimated $1.4 trillion deposited in tax havens abroad by Indians. The movements appear to have failed at the moment, but nevertheless have revealed hitherto unsuspected aspects of the citizens' thinking on the issue of corruption.

One common feature is the appeal to the moral principle of integrity in public life. While this can be easily understood the response of the political class showed that the very questioning of the activists and their demand for a role in the drafting of the bill was perceived as a case of the citizens challenging the right of the elected representatives in legislatures to draft and frame laws. This was their exclusive domain.

The activists were able to break through this conceptual barrier because the division of power between the Congress President Sonia Gandhi and the professional expert Dr Manmohan Singh as the head of the government in UPA after the 2004 election created a space for activists advising Sonia Gandhi to present their point of view. She was the wielder of real political power. The role of these activists led to significant legislation like the Right To Information Act, the NREGA (National Rural Employment Guarantee Act) etc.

Therefore when Team Anna and India Against Corruption activists demanded a role in drafting the Jan Lokpal Bill, the government could not resist it on principle for long. The exercise at best was with mixed results and was a failure.

The controversies accompanying the drafting of the Jan Lokpal Bill brought out issues of perception that the activists were challenging the democratic role of the elected representatives in framing the law for governance of the country.

The second issue that got highlighted was perhaps not anticipated. All political parties were exposed to be suffering from the same degree of indulging in corrupt practices. All were naked in the Hamam of politics. No one could claim to be morally cleaner than the rest.

What is worse even the integrity of the activists was being challenged. While the repeated strategy of threatening fasts and fixing deadlines ultimately led to the failure of the Anna Hazare movement, the Baba Ramdev movement lost its credibility when its own financial transactions were challenged. One point that got highlighted during the entire exercise was this – while the political parties were focusing on the ground realities and trying to compromise and get something positive on the ground, the activists increasingly took a theoretical stand. Just recall that in the Jantar Mantar days of 2011 Anna Hazare fast political leaders were specifically kept out!

If the essence of democracy is dialogue and compromise the activists in principle were 'anti-democratic'. The recent strategy of Kejriwal group of Team Anna to form a political party – Aam Aadmi Party – will be an interesting exercise to watch. The party will have to examine to what extent it will compromise so far as its attempt at punishing acts of corruption is concerned.

Does this mean that in a democracy like ours anti-corruption movements are bound to fail because they do not accept the essence of democracy of dialogue and compromise? Further if we start compromising on principles is it possible to have any check on corruption at all?

These are issues that need to be resolved.

We have to watch how the current anti-corruption movement ultimately evolves and what lasting contribution it can make to make our public life cleaner.

One thing is obvious. While in politics it may not be possible to achieve zero corruption, there are other sectors like the bureaucracy, judiciary, media etc where depending upon the type of moral leadership provided by the role models in these sectors, a higher degree of cleanliness can be achieved. Under the current circumstances that is perhaps the best hope we can entertain.

This is because sectoral leaders in different areas like judiciary, bureaucracy, corporate business and judiciary can hold on to and practice a higher degree of integrity. Therein lies our hope.

## IS POLITICAL SOLUTION THE ONLY ANSWER TO FIGHT CORRUPTION?

We are witnessing an interesting experiment in the Indian political scene today. Arvind Kejriwal has taken upon himself the task of building a brand new political party focused exclusively on ushering probity in public life. He has not given a name for his party, but has started with naming, shaming and exposing the acts of corruption by the powers that be across the political spectrum.

He is part of a tradition of similar efforts made in the past. A quick look at some of them:

1. An immediate predecessor is Dr Jayaprakash Narayan (IAS, 1980, Andhra Pradesh cadre). He is an idealist and a qualified doctor and took upon himself the task of fighting corruption at the grassroots. After 20 years in the IAS he resigned and organized a NGO called Lok Satta. He began with checking malpractices at the petrol pumps. Working quietly and systematically, he gradually spread his efforts across the whole of Andhra Pradesh. His NGO Lok Satta, attracted a lot of followers and soon ran into a lakh. He realized that governance cannot improve and corruption cannot be checked if criminals wield political power. His NGO therefore focused on the issue of criminals being nominated for elections to local bodies. It tried to persuade the political parties not to nominate candidates with criminal records. Even if such criminals were nominated and got elected they also focused on preventing such people occupying official positions in the local bodies. In course of time he converted the NGO into a regular political party. Lok Satta contested 2009 elections for the Andhra Pradesh legislature. Dr Jayaprakash Narayan became a member of the Assembly. He is a member of the National Advisory Council and has been exerting his influence through for good governance. Age is on his side and he may one day make a difference in public life.

2. In Tamil Nadu, where corruption has become endemic, idealist NRIs with IIT education a few years ago launched at the time of the State assembly elections in 2011, a party – Lokparitran – to make clean candidates contest the elections. Unfortunately the party itself soon become unravelled due to internal squabbles.
3. Undeterred by these failures the octogenarian associate of Mahatma Gandhi, V Kalyanam, who was his private secretary, has launched a party called National Protection Party – Desiya Padukappu Katchi – which is trying to educate the public about the need for integrity in public life and also contest elections, alas with poor results.
4. Anna Hazare's long crusade against corruption in Maharashtra is well-known.

All these efforts have had minimal impact in bringing about any significant change for the better. Never the less they have at least served the purpose of making a large number of people in the country sensitive to the dangers of corruption and lack of good governance.

In the ultimate analysis change has to come from within. Our democratic constitution has visualized certain agencies as to serve as watchdogs of governance with adequate powers. Three of them are in the constitution. These are the Judiciary, the Election Commission of India and the Comptroller and Auditor General of India. These can play a very effective role from within the system in ushering a corruption free governance in our country. Another organization is the statutory body – the Central Vigilance Commission.

Our system of governance will improve if the principle of appointing the right persons in the right posts is recognized. Our selection and appointment processes must be designed in such a way that every time this will happen almost automatically.

What we need therefore is to redesign our governance on the basis of the 2T principle. One T is for transparency with regards to qualifications, selection procedure and appointment of people to posts. The second T is ensuring that the process of selection itself is such that There Is No Alternative (TINA) but to select the right person for the post.

In the current nationwide debate on corruption there seems to be a consensus that only political solutions will work. But is this view correct? I am sceptical. Every party has a vested interest in the current system of governance. Why should they commit harakiri?

Changes can be brought about by a combination of constitutional and statutory bodies the bureaucracy, civil society organisations and the media.

Using these agencies and this principle may be the surest way of bringing about the desirable change without trying to create a party exclusively devoted to the principle of fighting corruption.

## REVOLT OF THE RURAL ELITE

On August 25, 2015, Ahmedabad – the premier city of Gujarat, witnessed a mind-boggling scene. There was a crackdown on members of the Patel community who were agitating for reservation in Government jobs and for benefits in education.

Hardik Patel, the 22-year-old youth who was spearheading the campaign, was also arrested and was subsequently released. The incident triggered massive violence and unrest in Gujarat with curfew imposed in several towns across the State. This event represents an important development in the evolution of post-Independence India. The freedom struggle was initially started by the English educated middle class consisting of lawyers, teachers and doctors in the late nineteenth century. After more than six decades of Independence, we are witnessing another stage of revolt. The middle class revolt in urban areas was dramatically highlighted by the Arvind Kejriwal phenomenon and the access to power of the AAP in Delhi, not once in 2013 but most decisively in 2014. Hardik Patel, who is only 22, has emerged as a powerful leader of perhaps the most powerful community in Gujarat Although he is leading the agitation in the urban city of Ahmedabad, he is the face of the rural elite. At the time of drafting the Constitution, Dr Ambedkar was able to articulate the need for reservation for depressed classes. He represented mainly the cause of the Dalits. But at the same time the special needs of the tribals who are mostly forest dwellers were also appreciated by the framers of the Constitution. Even though in the Fundamental Rights Chapter, reservation for Scheduled Castes and Scheduled Tribes was provided, it was considered to be only a temporary phenomenon, not expected to last beyond 15 years. Over time the reservations have got crystallized into almost a permanent feature of the Constitution. The Mandal agitation in the '70s and '80s led to the next social phenomenon of the OBCs which though surprisingly dominant in rural areas, managed to get more than 20% of the openings in education and government jobs reserved for them.

So far as Gujarat is concerned, in 1985, it was the Patels who opposed the reservation of posts for the OBCs. It is ironic that in 2015 it is the same Patels who are clamouring for a reservation in education access as well as government jobs for themselves.

This is an important development. Hardik represents the next stage in the evolution of society through revolt by a large and key section. He wants reservation for his community but fundamentally he is against the principle of reservation both in access to education and in jobs. While he sees social justice so far as reservation for weaker sections of society for access to education, he argues that reservation in government jobs including subsequent promotions is highly unjust, especially to communities like his (Patel), who are denied reservation both in access to education and in government jobs. Basically like Kejriwal whose single point was elimination of corruption, Hardik is calling for the focus on the economic criteria so far as access to education is concerned and merit when it comes to jobs.

In the long run the movement of Hardik represents a welcome step in the evolution of India into a modern socially just society. Let us not forget that Patels are not the first set of rural elite to revolt. The Jats in Haryana, Marathas in Maharashtra, Meenas in Rajasthan and the Yadavs in Uttar Pradesh and Bihar have preceded them. Interestingly both Kejriwal and Hardik are products of the digital communication revolution. Both have cleverly exploited its leverage potential for multiplier effect and derived full benefits using the global impact of social media or should we say the age of SCAM (Social, Cloud Analytic and Mobile Digital media).

## TWO AGITATIONS – TWO STRATEGIES

Two subjects had grabbed the attention of the nation and the media in the last two years – massive corruption scams and the protest of the civil society organizations against them. Anna Hazare and Baba Ramdev have emerged as two leaders guiding these protest movements. Each has a different strategy.

Anna Hazare evoked the Gandhiji strategy of a fast and Baba, the emotional appeal of the spiritual guru. But is that all? Is Baba following another unarticulated strategy also drawing on a precedent in our freedom struggle?

It appeared for some time that these protests may lead to some lasting changes for the better in our system of governance. Alas, as of August 2012 it appears that both these movements have failed. Anna was the first to lose his steam. His frequent threats of going on fast became somewhat like the case of the boy who cried 'wolf' too many times. The latest is the split in Team Anna and the search for a political option to fight corruption.

Gandhiji was perhaps the most successful leader we have had in our country when it comes to leading movement by civil societies. He realized the inherent asymmetry of power between the government or the establishment and organizations of citizens who challenged them. He drew his strategic insight from judo – the Japanese style of unarmed combat. The basic strength of judo is the converting of the enemy's strength into his weakness and taking advantage of it. Gandhiji's invention of the Satyagraha was a masterstroke in political judo. The British found that they could not fight this and ultimately lost.

Netaji Bose was another great leader of the freedom struggle who adopted the opposite strategy. He chose to challenge the British on their own terms – through arms. Taking advantage of the situation towards the end of World War II when the British were losing against the Japanese in Asia, he raised a regular army from the Indian prisoners of war and wrote an interesting chapter in India's freedom struggle. He was able to inspire a lot of Indians but ultimately his disappearance became a mystery and the source of endless conspiracy theories.

There are people who claim that the British finally left not because of Gandhiji's Satyagraha and the Quit India movement that he led but because the British knew that after the 1946 mutiny in the naval dockyard in Bombay they could not hold India any longer. A former acting Governor of West Bengal has cited Lord Clement Attlee himself in support of this view.

In a modern replay of the two strategies, if Anna's inspiration came from Mahatma Gandhi, Baba Ramdev seems to have subconsciously adopted the Netaji strategy. He has chosen to seek the support of the political parties opposed to the ruling party in his campaign to fight corruption and retrieve humungous amounts of black money stashed abroad in tax havens.

We will be witnessing both the campaigns which will gain increasing political relevance till the general elections of 2014. Only after this we can be sure which strategy is going to succeed.

Geopolitical factors like World War II created the environment for India's independence. Will the civil society movements led by Anna and Baba Ramdev in the context of the electoral battle to be fought in 2014, create an environment for a cleaner India? I wonder.

## EVOLUTION OF THE DIALOGUE OF PROTEST

Protest is the dialogue of communication so far as the governance of a State or society is concerned. Violence has traditionally been the basic language of protest. This is a language which every individual in a society understands readily. When public buildings of the government are burnt, means of public transport like buses and trains are damaged and mayhem is unleashed on society, greatly disturbing the functioning of disturbing the peace of vital institutions like schools and hospitals, a strong signal goes to the society, that there is something wrong with the system. It is also a sad fact that many governments do not take any corrective action unless such massive damage is done to society.

Depending upon the level of development and the system of governance the degree of violence will vary. In recent times we have seen the massive struggle for independence of India led by Mahatma Gandhi who adopted the unusual weapon of *ahimsa* and *satyagraha* to convince the British that they should leave India. The colonial rulers in South Africa were perhaps not as evolved in political sensitivity as the British in India, hence a great leader like Nelson Mandela had to face imprisonment for 27 long years and the blacks who were the dominant majority in the population had to suffer inhuman treatment under apartheid. This practice was universally condemned and the South African regime was severely isolated in the comity of nations. Finally the humane techniques of struggle adopted by Mandela and the African National Congress prevailed. South Africa was fortunate that Mandela took the responsibility and was able to govern during the transition period from colonial rule to democratic governance.

The explosion of revolutions and regime changes called the Arab Spring, witnessed from 2010 in the Middle-East starting with Egypt and on to Libya and Syria, has exposed the consequences of regime changes arising from the protest of the governed. The experience of the nearly 60 countries under the communist regimes from the late '90s showed that regime change and the collapse of the totalitarian regimes did not lead to a universal pattern of real democracy emerging peacefully. What had resulted ultimately in these countries is crony capitalism. Hopefully as has happened in Germany where the two parts of the country – East and West, got united is the best model to hope for.

These events in the late 20th and early 21st century underline some basic facts about the dynamics of the regime changes.

1. There is a craving for real democracy where the citizens ultimately take the initiative for policy choices. This in turn calls for institutionalizing the channel for communication between the governing State and the citizens who are governed.
2. Every society has to compulsorily go through the learning curve to realize good governance.
3. The language of protest evolves through a spectrum of violence, peaceful resistance and rational dialogue

between the governing State and the citizens to arrive at mutually satisfactory and stable equilibrium.

Thus, the democratic dialogue in Indian politics has opened a dramatic new chapter. Political protest will never be like the past. 2014 indeed marks a landmark in the development of Indian democracy.

## IS MODI A NON-RESIDENT PM?

As Prime Minister Narendra Modi enters his third year in office, one general point of criticism is that he is proving to be a non-resident PM rather than the Prime Minister of India.

An additional point of criticism is that the enormous time and money invested by him and the Government of India in these visits abroad have yielded little in terms of investment, employment generation, technology and economic development. It all appears to be only hype.

Non-Resident Indians seem to be keen on getting the best of both worlds. Their immediate goal was getting bureaucratic hurdles and red tape removed in matters like visa and travel restrictions as well as remittance of money. Their medium-term goal was getting the advantage of dual citizenship, ultimately resulting in voting rights – if not at least representation in the Rajya Sabha through nominated members. As NRIs have spread all over the world, their goal appears to be to have at least seven such nominations, one for each continent.

During his visits abroad, Modi has blazed a new trail in emulating the rockstars with professional event managements rivalling brand building efforts in the commercial sector. Has this led to building of brand India or brand Modi? The critics hold that it has been more building brand Modi rather than brand India.

The next point of criticism is that politically Modi himself and the BJP are facing the challenge of the weakening of the Modi wave and the erosion of the Modi magic. In 2014 Modi's magic won the States of Maharashtra, Haryana and Jharkhand for the BJP. Year 2015 was an unmitigated disaster. The BJP lost the Delhi and Bihar Assembly elections badly.

### Are these Criticisms Valid?

I think the critics are missing the basic fact that Modi is systematically building a successful track record so far as his strategy is concerned. Modi's tours of practically most of the countries in India's neighbourhood as well as the leading powers of the world in his first and second years have decisively demonstrated that he does not suffer from tunnel vision.

In fact, his hyped-up visits focused on NRIs in every country he visited were a totally new phenomenon. No other Prime Minister before him had set such a track record. So far as the medium-term impact of the visits is concerned, Modi has been able to establish personal rapport with the leaders of the world inspite of the fact that as Gujarat Chief Minister he was denied visa to the United States.

Has he diminished brand India's image and carried local politics to the global stage? Has he strayed away from the unwritten rule that in democracies leaders visiting foreign countries do not display their complaints on domestic political issues?

The overall result of his visits seems to be that Modi has won the goodwill of the non-resident Indians. This he has achieved by walking his talk and actually delivering the results. The red tape in the way of NRIs and citizens of Indian origin visiting India and investing here has been broadly removed. Thus one argument for the NRIs not matching the performance of the overseas Chinese has been removed.

Modi is fully aware of the virtuous cycle of non-resident Gujaratis investing in the State and contributing to employment generation, transfer of technology and economic development. He is trying to reproduce the impact of the experience of Gujarat at the level of the nation. The year 2016 was the critical year of Modi's current term and he is fully geared to meet the challenges of the next year and lay the firm foundation for success.

## OXYMORON POLITICS

One area where Narendra Modi has left a distinct mark as a non-Congress Prime Minister is of foreign relations.

India's first Prime Minister, Jawaharlal Nehru, had established his unique place in the area of foreign relations ever since he joined the freedom struggle. He always had a global vision unlike many of his compatriots who perceived themselves as the children of Mother India, which was tragically under the yoke of foreign rulers, the British.

We get a clear perception of Jawaharlal Nehru's view of the world in the series of letters he wrote to his daughter, Indira Priyadarshini, from prison in the 1930s which were ultimately published as *Glimpses of World History*.

Nevertheless, one can see distinctly Nehru's emerging fascination with the Fabian socialism of Sidney and Beatrice Webb which attracted the admiration of the one and the only dramatist, George Bernard Shaw.

Nehru who kept in touch with the emerging currents of political thought on the global scene was a committed Leftist when he became the Prime Minister of India. He naturally seized the opportunity conferred on him by destiny to build a Socialist Pattern of society in India. But soon he discovered he could not have his way.

He had to modify his strategy when he tried to introduce co-operative farming in the Avadi Resolution of the Congress session in 1953 but his commitment to the socialistic concept prevailed. Although the intentions of Nehru and his colleagues like Mahalanobis were noble and sincere, the net results on the ground were by and large negative, and totally different.

The Leftist bias of Jawaharlal Nehru continued by Indian rulers all these years till 2014, when Narendra Modi formed the first authentic non-Congress Right of the Centre Government. Although Nehru died in 1964, his influence so far as India's external affairs were concerned remained the dominant posture of India's foreign policy.

Modi's critics find many points to criticize his style of governance and the area naturally is India's relations with other countries. They still perceive Modi to be a State level political leader who has no direct experience in dealing with the world of diplomacy and whose vision is limited to Gujarat. Modi has now completed more than two years as Prime Minister and if there is an area where he has left a distinct stamp is handling India's Foreign Relations. He has been globe trotting to such an extent that critics call him a non-resident Prime Minister, especially after his surprising halt at Lahore to greet Pakistan Prime Minister Nawaz Sharif on his granddaughter's wedding. Modi's critics point out that such a policy amounts to a U-turn and a personalized approach to global issues is not the correct way to conduct diplomacy. The critics say that PM's visit must be planned well in advance since his visit to Lahore only acted as a meaningless exercise in political optics.

Coming to think of it the critics are asking Modi to be traditional and not be innovative at all. After all the years when Indian diplomacy was conducted according to the standard operating procedure under UPA rule, we are still left with a stalemate with Pakistan. Modi's thinking out of the box shows that he has escaped the Catch 22 situation. If he follows the procedure adopted so far, he will get nowhere. If he does something new as he has been doing, he is criticized for being naïve.

This is because his critics want him to fail. By laying down conditions of diplomacy that is standard operating procedure and at the same time demanding new initiatives and breakthroughs is a sheer case of trying to trap Modi in oxymoron politics. Unfortunately for them Modi has been too clever.

## ASSESSMENT OF THE MODI GOVERNMENT

I came across an article 'Modi One Year On' which refers to American think-tank Hudson Institute's assessment of Modi government's one year in office. The article says,

> "In its first year, the Modi government failed to live up to that expectation. Instead it appears to rely heavily on the bureaucracy for policy guidance, rather than demanding that civil servants put the political leaders' ideas into effect.... The BJP-led government was voted into power by a new generation of Indians. The new Indian electorate is aspirational and demands instant gratification and immediate results. Modi's other backer, domestic and foreign business, is also impatient for positive results. Markets run on sentiments and until now the upswing in Indian economic growth has been primarily because the markets remain hopeful of change for the better. Prime Minister Modi must act fast before this hopefulness dissipates."

Is this assessment correct? Is there some aspect that is missing?

As an old civil servant my take is that this account does not appreciate the realities of the internal dynamics of the Indian political system that has evolved since Independence.

It is true that we inherited the British model for governance with the permanent civil service. But over the years the Indian system of governance has developed its own strengths and weaknesses. The strengths like handling the unprecedented bloodshed of the Partition, meeting the challenge of more than 10 million refugees from East Pakistan in 1970, and repeatedly handling the challenges of natural and man-made disasters like floods and famine are not considered achievements at all. Even the three great revolutions – the Green Revolution, the White (Milk) Revolution and the Blue (Space and Nuclear energy) Revolution – are taken for granted.

It is only the failures of the bureaucracy-corruption and red tape associated with it – that are constantly highlighted. This distortion is also reflected in the assessment of the Hudson Institute.

For a badly-needed corrective just consider the following:

> Although ideally political leadership frames the policy, its execution on the ground has to be only through the bureaucracy. No leader however competent he may be can by himself do the work of execution in a country like ours of subcontinental dimensions. I had a boss who used to say that a bad master is one who keeps a dog and does the barking himself. Does that mean that the Government has become totally dependent on the bureaucracy?

Modi and his team are very clear about their objectives and fundamental ideology. They are certainly not looking to the bureaucracy for policy guidance. In fact, the main achievement of the Modi government is the great tectonic change it has brought in the philosophy and ideology of governance. From 1947 it has been Left of the Centre. The establishment intelligentsia is shocked and is still in a state of denial. It has yet to realize that the patronage of the State it enjoyed all these years may no longer be automatic and a given.

In the last one year, foundations have been laid by the Modi government from where the economy can be given a boost even without big ticket headlines grabbing actions like the failure of getting passed legislation on land acquisition for infrastructure projects.

Equally important is labour legislation where again some States like Rajasthan have already taken the lead.

The economy at the end of one year of the Modi government has created enough potential to get out of the trap of policy paralysis of the previous government which it inherited. The best course, therefore, would be for all players in the economy and governance to take a positive and activist approach instead of being armchair critics.

## NIRMAL GANGA: UNIQUE SWADESHI SOLUTION

Ganga, the supreme river of India has caught the imagination of the whole nation in a very dramatic fashion these days. In politics, Narendra Modi made it the central emotional pivot covering politics, culture, heritage and national pride. Restoring a *nirmal* (clean) and *aviral* (free-flowing) Ganga has taken on an urgency and priority which has never been witnessed in the past.

The Supreme Court recently expressed the frustration of the people of India when it made very sharp comments about the action taken over the last 3 decades and more. Enough of vision statements and objectives, enough of long detailed expert committee reports. On 24th September 2014, the Supreme Court wanted the Government of India to present an affidavit along with its power point presentation on a time bound action plan to clean and rejuvenate the Ganga.

And there is an excellent news: An Indian engineer and scientist – Dr Rajah Vijay Kumar, chief of the Organization de Scalene, a research setup based in Bangalore – has come up with a unique solution which is mind-blowing and sounds like magic. As has been said all advanced technology looks like magic.

Dr Vijay Kumar, a 100% Indian, has come up with a very original, out-of-the-box solution. He holds 27 international patents. His solution to the problem of pollution in water whose basic principles are listed below, have been demonstrated successfully in the city of Bangalore and the coffee estate owned by the Wadias in Coorg. It is to be applied for tackling the problem of pollution in a 750 km long river in Mexico from January 2015. In Netherlands, this technology is being applied to tackle the problems of big pharma companies that are stymied by the government ban on discharging their effluents in any water body.

## What is Pollution?

### *Principle 1*

In the ultimate analysis it is the suspension of particles of varying size from microns to nano in a medium – liquid or air. As the particles are electrically negative on the surface and positive at the centre, they repel each other. If the negative charge could be neutralized by bombarding with electro-magnetic waves of 8 mega Hertz to 12 mega Hertz, they collapse and tend to form clots. This is called thrombosis. All of us are familiar with the problem of the clotting of blood in the arteries resulting in coronary thrombosis.

In short this is the heart of Dr Vijay Kumar's technology. He named his machine as Aquatron or Fine Particle Shortwave Thrombolytic Agglomeration Reactor (FPSTAR). He has in a sense managed to deliver a heart attack to the all pervasive problem of pollution.

Just as the boiling of the tea kettle triggered James Watt's mind to invent the steam engine in the 18th century, coronary thrombosis has triggered Dr Vijay Kumar's mind for solving the problem of pollution.

*Principle 2*

The second major principle of this technology is to focus on the problem in a decentralized fashion. All these years we have allowed the problem of pollution to grow and grow in size and taken note only after it became a giant. Dr Vijay Kumar's approach is to nip the problem in the bud. According to the current plan, if all goes well, his technology will be demonstrated in 2 places – Okhla where the Yamuna enters Delhi and is fed by 7 nullahs or streams carrying polluted water and also the sewage from nearly 60 slums along the river bank. The second place would be Varanasi which is the centre of attraction in the major effort launched by the Modi government. In that city the two rivers – Varuna and Ashi, after which the city is named will be taken up for demonstrating the technology along with three or four slums.

So far as the slums are concerned, Dr Vijay Kumar's technology claims that within a period of 4-6 weeks, the sewage water can be treated and brought up to pollution free status and there will be no need for discharging the water into sewage system. The treated water can be recycled and used for gardening and other purposes. Dr Vijay Kumar claims that it can even be drinkable though there may be a certain level of squeamishness in making tea out of treated sewage water. So far as the streams and rivers are concerned, there will be a need of installing reactors of the appropriate size where the thrombosis of the polluted particles takes place and is further treated to make them free of toxicity.

There is a high degree of confidence in the time lines given and the results because this has already been demonstrated both in the Scalene campus in Bangalore and the coffee estate in Coorg. The international patent has been given after due scrutiny and diligence.

The next major step is scaling up and crossing the tipping point for the entire effort to take off on a massive scale. Looking to the various initiatives taken by the Modi government it should not be difficult to systematically organize public-private participation, spanning Central Government, State Governments, NGOs and activists. It will be one more demonstration of ultimately finding an eco-friendly, humane solution to a global threat. Thanks to the initiative of Al Gore, the inconvenient truth about environmental degradation has become conventional wisdom all over the world. The Indian solution to the Ganga problem can be the new beacon pointing the way to a bright future.

To ensure that industries like tanneries, textiles, paper, dyes which are on the river-banks and cause pollution not only in the Ganga but other rivers are tackled, Dr Vijay Kumar has developed industry specific solutions which have been demonstrated in the Scalene campus. Hence zero discharge from industries as well as cities and villages is something that can be realized effectively.

In other words, with this new vision there will be no need for massive pipelines, chemicals and huge investment. The Supreme Court can hopefully see the benefits of Nirmal Ganga in the next 5 years on the outside and not 200 years.

## A SURE-FIRE STRATEGY FOR SUCCESS IN REALIZING NIRMAL/AVIRAL GANGA AND SWACHH BHARAT

Achieving success within a defined time period of say 20 years and make Nirmal/Aviral Ganga and Swachh Bharat a reality and not an ever receding dream calls for solving the following problems:

1. **Sewage and Effluents:** Liquid waste polluting Ganga is in two forms – sewage and effluents (industry and others). Sewage amounts to 12,000 MLD and forms 80% of the quantity. Effluents amount to 3,000 MLD (20%). The most dangerous form of pollution in the liquid form when it comes to toxicity and damage to human and other forms of life are the effluents (industrial and otherwise).

   Although effluents constitute 20% in terms of quantity they are the cause of 80% of toxicity and damage. In the case of sewage there is no single point in governance at city/municipal levels. In many places there are no sewage networks. Even where they exist they may be old and ineffective.

   When it comes to effluents, less than 30% is treated and that too, very poorly. Water is treated as a free natural resource by the industry. Hence there is no incentive to save on the quantity of water used.

2. **Maintaining Ecological and Geological Integrity of the Ganga:** This can be achieved by ensuring that there is always a water flow in the river in terms of the environmental and geological flow. Environmental

> flows means the regime of flows including sediments and other natural constituents to maintain the ecological integrity of a river and the goods and services provided by it computed by building (Bigger) block method. Geologic entity is an entity formed by ancient earth processes over geologic ages. In short maintaining the environmental and geological integrity means ensuring environmental flows and preserving geological entity.

Fortunately as the government launches the Nirmal/Aviral Ganga and the Swachh Bharat programmes, we can visualize a surefire strategy for success. Basic technologies are available and utilizing them through an imaginative scheme involving public-private participation is very much in the realm of possibility.

This can be the main instrument for success. This reluctance of the polluters can overcome by enacting laws to make it mandatory that polluters must pay.

That is not all. Even the reluctant ones can adopt a new Swadeshi technology developed by an Indian scientist from Bengaluru Dr Rajah Vijay Kumar. This is called FPSTAR and has been awarded an international patent by the EU in December 2013. FPSTAR stands for Fine Particle Shortwave Thrombolytic Agglomeration Reactor. Any polluted water is a liquid medium in which fine particles are suspended. As they are in the range of microns that have a negative charge on the surface. The unique feature of the technology is that it does not use any chemicals or radioactive material and cost-wise it is the cheapest among all the existing technologies so far as pollution treatment is concerned. While other technologies do not treat the problem of removing toxicity, this technology does. The technology is inspired by the same process which leads humans to suffer coronary thrombosis or myocardial infarction.

What about the sewage? This has to be funded by the government as the State is responsible for ensuring infrastructure for public health. Innovative financial engineering like issuing Ganga bonds can be adopted.

These bonds can be like Kisan Vikas Patras introduced in the past. Any person can invest cash in these without being required to declare the source of funds. With minimum dependence on the consolidated fund of India the core of the Swachh Bharat and Nirmal/Aviral Ganga can be implemented.

## MAINTAINING ECOLOGICAL AND GEOLOGICAL INTEGRITY

The application of FPSTAR technology can help greatly to use the fresh water. By fixing a market sensitive price for water the large users of fresh water may incentivized to drastically reduce the amount of fresh water. This will make maintaining environmental and geological flows a manageable and tractable problem.

The FPSTAR technology so far as treatment of urban solid waste is concerned is being demonstrated in New Delhi in the Okhla area under NDMC. The using of this technology for treatment of sewage and effluents is also being demonstrated in the Okhla NDMC area of Delhi Jal Board.

Within the next six months the results will become public and the impact of the unique technology with an imaginative scheme for PPP, may prove to be the silver bullet that will meet the challenge of Nirmal/Aviral Ganga and Swachh Bharat in the period 2014-2019.

# 6

# National Security

## ENSURING A YOUNGER LEADERSHIP FOR DRDO

Dinesh C Sharma, writing in *Business Line* on 15th January 2015 says,

> "The sacking of Avinash Chander, head of the Defence Research and Development Organisation, has shaken the world of scientific research. Coming on the heels of the delayed appointment of a new chief for the Indian Space Research Organisation and continuing ad hocism at the Council of Scientific and Industrial Research, it points to the larger issue of how our top scientific agencies function and how the government handles them. The explanation given by the defence minister is pathetic. He says DRDO needs a younger leadership. What it and other scientific agencies actually need is a complete overhaul. A full blueprint for DRDO's reform has been ready and waiting since 2010."

Here are some ideas which can be easily implemented given the commitment of the Modi government for national security and the most refreshing and unique Defence Minister, India has had since Independence in 1947 – Dr Manohar Parrikar.

There has never been a more brilliant, intellectually sharp and active minister who has already built an excellent track record in good governance. There has never been a more focused, result-oriented minister like him in the Ministry of Defence so far.

Fortunately we need not start from zero. A lot of work has already been done. A well-thought-out and pragmatic report of the panel headed by Dr P Rama Rao has already been submitted to the Government of India in 2008 and is gathering dust. This report itself can be the starting point. The panel recommendations included decentralising the DRDO management and merging some of its labs with other public funded labs working in similar areas, overhauling its human resources policy and establishing a commercial arm for technology business.

One should not however get a feeling that the various defence ministers in the past 20 years since the historic liberalisation measures introduced by the Narasimha Rao government with the able support of Dr Manmohan Singh, have been totally ineffective.

Even Sharma concedes –

> "In the past 15 years, India has witnessed a great expansion of its science and technology infrastructure with new departments and institutions being established. The expansion of the IITs and rolling out of the Indian Institutes of Science Education and Research are part of this wave of institution building. Budgetary support for

scientific departments has increased substantially. The funding for scientific departments (agriculture research not included) during the Eleventh Plan was about ₹59,000 crore. It is projected to more than double to ₹1,42,000 crore during the Twelfth Plan period."

The Defence Minister has put his finger on the key weakness of the MOD – lack of young leadership. The challenge is how to attract the youth and that too the most creative and sharp scientific minds which are research oriented. Here are some ideas:

1. The youth who join the DRDO and do research must be entitled to have the intellectual property rights in their own name which in turn will become a key incentive. The US for instance has a special law passed in the 1980s to realize this. There is no reason why India cannot duplicate or adopt this precedent.
2. The movement between the scientists in the DRDO and the industry which is interested in exploiting the IPR must be freely allowed. It may be recalled that during the World War II, the British government allowed members of the Indian Civil Service and other government servants including engineers to be seconded to the Tata Steel at Jamshedpur. There is a special provision in the Conduct Discipline Appeals rule for Central Government for this.
3. New models of public-private partnership conceived imaginatively in which every participant including the society at large, benefits, must be implemented without getting trapped in rules and regulations. This was the concept initially of the special economic zones.

Even these ideas will bring about a dramatic change visualized by the Defence Minister and ensure that DRDO becomes a vibrant creative organization.

With these radical changes the next step is implementing more or less in toto the Dr Rama Rao panel recommendations.

With Dr Parrikar at the helm, DRDO a world beater.

## OROP: NAMO'S MGR MOMENT

As PM, NaMo has set many records in terms of being the first unique PM in India. I am an unabashed admirer of our PM.

The Independence Day speech delivered by the Prime Minister from the historic ramparts of the Red Fort in Delhi has a unique resonance. The venue and the long history of the place always reminds me of the immortal words of Napoleon addressing his French troops at the foot of the pyramids – 2,000 years of history are looking down on you.

The PM's speech reminds me of the great and not-so-great leaders who have addressed the nation in the last 68 years since Independence. NaMo has stamped his unique brand on the I-Day speeches. His first speech last year was memorable in many aspects.

This year's speech also came up to my expectations but there was one major disappointment. The media had speculated that OROP (One Rank One Pension) demand of the ex-servicemen had become a time bomb which was only becoming more complicated as every day passed by. I was half expecting that the PM would display his unique trait for springing surprises and would score a historic sixer by announcing the government's decision on this critical issue which has defied a solution for more than two decades.

In politics, there are various types of problems and challenges. OROP is one of those rare cases where a bold leap to judgment is triggered by a political leader to smash through the policy paralysis on resolving such issues.

Policy paralysis in bureaucracy arises from the obvious fact that there are many clever, intelligent, knowledgable and competent people occupying key positions. They contribute their concepts and participate in the evolution of policy. This provides an excellent breeding ground for turf battles and ego clashes.

In the ultimate analysis, it all boils down to a basic process of the better becoming the enemy of the good. One expert may come up with a good solution which would resolve the issue but another will come up with a better one. In the resulting clash of views a search is launched for yet another solution and so on.

In such situations one of the oldest examples of finding the solution goes back to the legend of Alexander the Great cutting the Gordian knot. In our democratic system, the parallel is a popular bold political leader exercising his choice based on his intuition and innate or even subliminal understanding of what the people need and what would be popular, ensuring the eternal loyalty of the voters.

I am sure that NaMo is one of the clean, honest, great and highly competent popular leaders we have seen in recent times and he has in him the courage and capacity to emulate another leader in recent times. That leader is MGR, who ruled unchallenged as the CM of Tamil Nadu for 13 years in the '70s.

After retirement I have settled down in Tamil Nadu. In this State, MGR who was a very popular hero in films has become a legendary political leader who commands the heart and devotion of generations of the poor and especially women. Apart from his many achievements both in politics and in films, what has made him unique is that he was the person who introduced the mid-day meals scheme for all school children without any restrictions. It was the visionary leader Kamaraj who introduced the idea of providing the mid day meals to the poor but it was MGR who expanded it to the entire community of students which was unheard of. My colleague and batchmate in the IAS, K Venkatesan, who was the Finance Secretary in that period recalled an anecdote about how MGR tackled the issue of policy paralysis arising from the enormous financial commitment facing the State, if his pet scheme of mid day meals for all schoolchildren was introduce. It seems MGR asked all the concerned officers who were raising objections from the point of view of finance, a simple question – Has any one of you ever suffered in your youth a situation where you were totally starving without food and did not know when and where your next meal would come from?

Naturally, none of the officers had faced such situations. Then MGR delivered his judgment –

> "As a boy I have faced that situation of total starvation. I can feel the pain of the poor hungry children. I therefore order you to go ahead and introduce the scheme."

That decision taken by MGR in the 1970s has brought excellent results. The World Bank which was in principle opposed to subsidies and freebies did a policy somersault when it found that the mid-day meal scheme not only improved attendance in school but also brought tangible, palpable positive social results by way of empowerment of women, the better control of family size and population, overall development in the quality of life for many below the poverty lie and so on. The very spread of education strengthened the roots of democracy.

OROP is a problem which poses to our Prime Minister his MGR moment. Will he rise to the occasion? I hope he does.

## TOWARDS CLEAN AND EFFECTIVE PROCUREMENT IN DEFENCE

The 'Choppergate' which the TimesNow news channel calls as the 'Armsgate' is the latest in the long history of major defence procurement scandals in our more than 6 decades of post-Independence history.

By their very nature there is a lot of secrecy about the whole issue of procurement for defence thanks to the angle of national security, high technology, limited number of players and the humungous amounts of money involved.

A big nation like India has to become more self-reliant in defence equipment. There is always a gap between the development of indigenous capacity for defence production and the need of the defence forces. The harsh reality today is that India is perhaps the largest importer of vital defence equipment and weapons in the world. We are also a vibrant and boisterous democracy. Today we are in the era of fractured politics and coalitions. The media and especially the electronic media, have become very effective in their presence and coverage. Every scandal generates a lot of attention. We have reached a stage where the common man has lost his faith in the government and is ready to believe that there is corruption involved in every major decision of the government which has financial implications. Even the wildest allegations are believed.

The agents of foreign manufacturers of defence equipment have emerged as the villains of the piece. This became so after the wide publicity generated in the context of the Bofors deal in the '80s. The government of Rajiv Gandhi which had a very clean image to begin with, imposed a total ban in 1989 on all Indian agents when it came to weapons procurement for defence forces. This resulted in the entire activity of defence agents becoming invisible officially. Nevertheless as is the global reality is that defence agents play a role in every country. As the Central Vigilance Commissioner, in the year 2000, I was asked to inquire into the allegation whether after the Government of India's ban in 1989 on middlemen in defence procurement, they continued to exist or not. I had to report that this was indeed true that inspite of the official ban the middlemen flourished in the area of defence procurement. I also recommended that the policy must be reviewed and looking to the legitimate services rendered by the agents, especially when it comes to arranging demonstrations, briefing about the weapon systems and servicing after delivering the equipment, agents indeed were required. In September 2001, the government revised its policy and laid down the conditions under which the defence agents can be registered. Unfortunately the conditions were so stringent that hardly anyone had been registered till I retired in 2002.

There is a tendency today to consider every activity of the defence agents as a case of corruption. Aryama Sundaram, a thoughtful Supreme Court lawyer came up with a very insightful comment in one of the umpteen discussions triggered by the current scandal of Choppergate. He highlighted the need for drawing a clear distinction between three activities – (1) lobbying, (2) getting a commission for services rendered, and (3) bribing. Lobbying is generally allowed in many countries. The dos and don'ts are well-known and strict action can be taken legally when there are violations. Commissions can also very clearly defined which would be for the services rendered by the agent like arranging for demonstrations, meetings, service after supply of equipment etc. Bribing takes place when a part of the money involved in the deal ends up in the pockets of the policy makers or the decision makers in the procurement process. This is dangerous and should be severely dealt with.

In recent years the continuous coverage of scams has led to an enormous trust deficit so far as the government is concerned. Can we not make a beginning towards a clean and effective procurement in defence based on the principles enunciated by Aryama Sundaram?

# 7

# Modi Doctrine and Balochistan

After coming to power in 2014, Modi government has been following very radically different policies from the previous governments in the past.

Perhaps the most dramatic articulation of the new diplomacy was the specific mention of India's support to the aspirations of Balochis for setting up an independent Balochistan in the Prime Minister Narendra Modi's independence day speech in 2016 delivered from the historic ramparts of the Red Fort.

What is the reason for this shift in policy?

Because, this is the first government which has an open commitment to the policies right of the centre and share values of our Bharatiya Sanskriti and the concept of Sanatana Dharma.

Even more important is the fact that it follows the Sanatana Dharma in practice.

This is indeed a major change in the ideology of governance post-1947. The classic articulation of that Dharma was demonstrated both in theory and practice by Vishnugupta who was also called Chanakya or Kautilya. He was the Dean of the Takshashila University in the north-west India (now in Pakistan) at the time of the invasion of Alexander the great. This event according to the western authors was somewhere around 325 BC, but according to Dr V Lakshmikantham who is a well-known professor of mathematics at the Florida Institute of Technology in Melbourne (Florida, USA), it was at least 1,500 years before it!

Dr Lakshmikantham is an expert in the field of non linear analysis. In his book *The Origin of Human Past: Children of Immortal Bliss* published by Bharatiya Vidya Bhavan in 1999, he opens for all of us hitherto unknown facts about our heritage and culture. For all of us brought up in the Macauley tradition of English education introduced by the British colonial government this book is indeed an eye opener.

Kautilya's *Arthashastra* is the pragmatic articulation of Sanatana Dharma for governance and politics including war and diplomacy. The most dramatic application of this was by Chanakya, when he guided Chandragupta Maurya to save our Bharat from the invasion of Alexander and build a long-lasting empire of the Mauryas.

And on Kautilya's advice, Chandragupta Maurya was able to build a first well-known huge empire in India. So far as Balochistan is concerned, it will fit in the Modi doctrine as an application of the four methods of *sama*, *dama*, *danda*, *bheda*.

From a historical point of view, much later on in the 17th century, the doctrine was adopted by Chhatrapati Shivaji under the advice of his guru Samartha Ramdas and earlier in the 14th century by Harihara and Bukka on the advice of their guru Vidyaranya.

There has always been a combination of a saint reflecting the Sanatana Dharma and the man of action like Chandragupta Maurya or Harihara and Bukka or Krishna Devaraya and Shivaji. This formula has been time tested over the period of more than thousand years. We can therefore nurture the hope that the current policy articulated by the Modi government has a possibility of success. It is likely to succeed better than the policies adopted in the past. The strength of the policy springs from it being in tune with the heritage of the country and its roots in the values of Sanatana Dharma.

It is in not only drawing inspiration from the cultural heritage and values of our ancient land but intelligently adopting them to the ever changing situations of diplomacy and politics that Narendra Modi has made his unique contribution.

As far as domestic politics are concerned, the very name Hinduism and RSS have been maligned and totally abused throughout the last 80 years of the existence of that organization by the secular intelligentsia starting with the band of label of fascism, the repeated attempts to spread the lie that Nathuram Godse who assassinated Mahatma Gandhi was a member of RSS, particularly singling out virulent attack on the concept of 'Hindutva' as articulated by Veer Savarkar. After all he was only following the tradition of some leaders in Hinduism who had emphasized on the need for resorting to violence if necessary to protect national dignity and integrity of Hinduism. The identification of Narendra Modi in his life from an impressionable age with the fundamental concept of Sanatana Dharma and applying them to the practical world of diplomacy has moulded him into a unique leader in the Indian political scene.

Consciously or unconsciously, Modi has followed the trail blazed by Chanakya who was able to impart the principles of Sanatana Dharma with real world of diplomacy and evolved techniques like sama, dama, danda, bheda. It may be recalled that Chanakya single-handedly identified Chandragupta Maurya after his father Suryagupta was treacherously assassinated by Mahapadmananda who was after all his barber. Television serial 'Chandra Nandini' of the popular TV channel Vijay Super is being a timely reminder for those who want to understand the significance of the emergence of the right of centre thinking all over the world, especially in India after the tectonic, which Narendra Modi has been able to articulate ever since he was able to seize power by leading the BJP in 2014.

As already mentioned, concept of Sanatana Dharma and the Kautilya *Arthashastra* have been tested over time. It is not surprising that the Modi doctrine is emerging as the right formula for the 21st century diplomacy.

It is interesting that the whole media was taken aback when Donald Trump emerged as the President of the United States in the Presidential election of 2016, the shock value of this emergence has been selected in an interesting article in *The Times of India*, Chennai edition, dated December 6, 2016 by Amulya Gopalakrishnan brought out power to the people down with the elites, the following extracts are interesting:

> "Everybody hates 'elites' these days. Demonetisation, with the economic turmoil it is wreaking might work out for Prime Minister Narendra Modi only if people feel that some rich persons somewhere, suffering more. BJP is trying its best to stoke this sentiment: the PM has reminded

> everyone of his 'Chaiwala' past, claiming to serve a strong brew that the poor liked, and the rich did not."
>
> "Right-wing chatter is full of conspiracy theories about how the opposition, the media and other Lutyen's forces are plotting to make demonetisation fail."
>
> "This case of mid is perfectly natural, given whom this party represents – the better-off are more likely to gravitate to BJP. It is still a dense bloc of class and caste privilege, despite its 2014 inroads into non-traditional groups."
>
> "So Modi's Robin Hood moves are not about bringing lasting gains for the poor. So far, nothing in his administrative record or his sources of support incline him in that direction either. Like all populist leaders, he just uses words to create a fog."

The adoption of the slogan, 'Ab ki bar Trump sarkar' promoted by People of Indian Origin (PIO) who came together as the Republican Hindus coalition to support him also brings out another interesting current political reality. This is the fact that even as the Modi government crosses the midpoint of its first term, the post-independence secular, politically correct intelligentsia in our country which has dominated the academic institutions and the media for all these seven decades since has not realized the tectonic impact and relevance wrought by Narendra Modi and his government in 2014 and thereafter.

The global perspective on this change is provided in his article by William H Avery, former United States diplomat and author. The Indian perspective is brought home by Ms Ishani Dattagupta in her article under the title, 'How Republican Hindu Coalition did their Bit to Help Donald Trump?'

We may begin with a global perspective to understand what were the driving forces which propelled Trump to the White House much against the vocal support and clear stands taken by many senior leaders of the Republican Party itself and the media projections favouring Hillary Clinton.

William H Avery, in his article 'After Donald Trump's Victory, Global Trade May Never be the Same Again', observes:

> "In Donald Trump American blue collar workers have found their Barack Obama, an inspiring figure who gives them hope for a better future. They just put Trump in the White House to deliver that better future. He will do that by abandoning the United States' long-standing commitment to increasingly free trade, in order to bring manufacturing jobs back home. With Trump's election global trade may well never be the same again."

When the Prime Minister announced dramatically on his Independence Day speech in 2016 about the dramatic shift in the policy India will adopt so far as the aspiration of the people of Balochistan are concerned, it send a very strong signal of a totally new strategic insight. If this is true, how is it different and what are the main factors?

Before we go further in this, we must take note of a very perceptive article written by Suhasini Haidar in the Opinion Lead article in *The Hindu*, Chennai Edition, dated December 10, 2016. In that article, she makes the following interesting points about the policy we adopted so far broadly regarding Pakistan, particularly regarding Balochistan.

> "In June this year, just after Prime Minister Narendra Modi's visit to Washington, a senior American official

spoke of the 'Modi Doctrine', giving formal recognition to the foreign policy choices adopted by India since May 2014. In his speech at the US Congress, Narendra Modi outlined India's commitment to the partnership with the US as being a 'new symphony in play' in order to build an international maritime partnership in Asia, to play a leading role in the South Asian neighbourhood, strategically as well as for humanitarian purposes, and to take a strong position on terrorism or cross-border terrorism emanating from Pakistan."

A few months later, Union External Affairs Minister Sushma Swaraj, speaking at the launch of a book *The Modi Doctrine: New Paradigms in India's Foreign Policy*, went on to define it thus: India first, neighbourhood first, engaging competing global powers, with a focus on the diaspora and on delivery.

## A TOUCH OF 'UNPREDICTABILITY'

It could be argued that none of these goals are new. While the shift from non-alignment to a US partnership began during Prime Minister Atal Bihari Vajpayee's tenure, the special maritime partnerships with Japan, Australia, the US and Singapore, as a response to China's assertiveness in the South China Sea, go back nearly a decade (2007). The focus on Pravasi Bharatiyas goes back even further.

In his own account of the 'Gujral doctrine', former Prime Minister IK Gujral articulated a 'SAARC minus Pakistan' neighbourhood approach when he said, "With neighbours like Bangladesh, Bhutan, Maldives, Nepal and Sri Lanka, India does not ask for reciprocity, but gives and accommodates what it can in good faith and trust." And in 2013, when former Prime Minister Manmohan Singh articulated his 'five-point' foreign policy objectives, he too put domestic development at the top: "The single most important objective of Indian foreign policy has to be to create a global environment conducive to the well-being of our great country."

At the half-way mark in Narendra Modi's term, after which governments traditionally turn from foreign policy to domestic elections, what then makes his foreign policy distinct? The answer to that may have come from Union Defence Minister Manohar Parrikar's comments in the past few months where he has repeatedly referred to the need for 'unpredictability' in India's defence, nuclear and strategic postures. It is easy to see that Narendra Modi's foreign policy thinking, which is 'out of the box', and taking all by surprise at every turn, has also incorporated this element, right since he invited South Asian leaders to his swearing-in ceremony in May 2014.

Since then, whether it was the sudden moment on a swing with Chinese President Xi Jinping, in Gujarat in 2014, the Republic Day invite to US President Barack Obama, in 2015, or the surprise stops in Kabul and Lahore on his return from Moscow last Christmas, the Prime Minister's foreign forays have had a shock-and-awe character. His closest partnership was forged with the US, the country that shut him out for nine years, while his biggest success came from Bangladesh, the country whose citizens he swore during his electoral campaign to shut out. He is yet to visit Israel, the country he spoke of most often as a friend, but he has completed several tours to West Asia – to the United Arab Emirates, Saudi Arabia, Qatar – and has already visited Iran, Israel's arch enemy. None of this could have been gamed in advance by even the keenest watchers of Narendra Modi or of the government's foreign policy.

## CROSSING RED LINES

With Pakistan that doctrine of unpredictability has been most pronounced. After more than a year of fits and starts, Narendra Modi decided to restart dialogue with Pakistan and pay a surprise visit to Lahore in December 2015, although the cancellation of India-Pakistan dialogue after the Pathankot attack was probably predictable. In 2016, he announced three strikes on Pakistan in quick succession. On Independence Day, he announced a new, activist policy towards Balochistan's freedom movement, a major departure from India's traditional policy of non-interference. Next came the announcement of cross-Line of Control strikes in retaliation for the Uri attacks, and a departure from India's policy of keeping such operations covert. Finally came the announcement along with neighbouring countries of a boycott of the SAARC (South Asian Association for Regional Cooperation) summit in Pakistan. If he makes good on the threat of abrogating or renegotiating the Indus Waters Treaty, as he seemed to indicate at an election rally in Punjab this month, then that will most certainly be his fourth strike, each one crossing a new red line.

It must be noted that each of these moves has been accompanied by considerable domestic applause and sometimes international approbation. With its obvious 'first-mover' advantages, this approach to staid, constrained and predictable foreign policy has given Narendra Modi some his most successful moments in the past two and a half years. The approach is also not without precedent, just as former US President Richard

Nixon – who called it the 'Madman Theory', according to his chief of staff Harry Haldeman's memoirs – told Henry Kissinger to convey to Russia and the Communist bloc that he was capable of any 'irrational' action (read nuclear) on Vietnam.

US President-elect Donald Trump too has often expressed his desire to be 'Nixonian' on Syria, North Korea, etc, in not allowing other countries to guess his future strategy. His recent surprise call to Taiwan's President indicates that he is going ahead with his version of the 'Madman Theory'. However, for a number of reasons – and not just because Vietnam didn't go as planned for Nixon – it is time to reassess the Modi government's dependence on the doctrine's value going forward.

## DANGER OF DIMINISHING RETURNS

To begin with, there is a law of diminishing returns that accompanies unpredictability, as the shock value of the government's manoeuvres wears off, and both adversaries and allies come to 'expect the unexpected'.

Second, not everyone likes surprises. China and Pakistan, most notably, can be expected to counter the doctrine with an overly aggressive defence posture, which would then lead to more tensions at India's frontiers just when the Modi government may want to focus on economic and domestic policies the most.

The recent spate of attacks on security installations in Jammu and Kashmir indicates that the Pakistani establishment was only momentarily **stunned by the 'surgical strikes'** announcement and more such attacks may be expected. A doctrine of unpredictability runs counter to the deterrence theory as well, which rests on the sure principle of what the response might be, nuclear or otherwise. This means that the response to a Uri-style attack would have to be something similar to September 29 or stronger, leaving India with very few non-war options.

India's policy of diplomatically isolating Pakistan may also suffer from this pushback as Pakistan steps up its efforts to engage China, Russia and Iran on connectivity, offering them strategic maritime advantages off its shores which it had not in the past.

Most importantly, a policy of unpredictability works best in an otherwise predictable global scenario. When Narendra Modi took office, oil prices were low, the dollar was stable, Europe was united and the US led by Barack Obama had set a steady, engaged course in Asia.

Today, none of those factors hold. The US under Donald Trump is likely to keep relations with India on the upward trajectory in strategic and defence fields but may not be able to deliver on Indian concerns on jobs and immigration. Moreover, should he deliver on his promise to pull out of the Trans-Pacific Partnership free trade agreement and to withdraw US resources from Asia and West Asia, it would change the power balance in this region in favour of China. Closer ties with Russia would also alter the power balance, given the Russia-China axis. As election after election springs a surprise, Britain's exit from the European Union may well be followed by Italy's exit from the Eurozone, the far right's entry to power in France and Germany, and a strain between the US and NATO.

"What will be the nature of western unity and will it be continued?," asked Foreign Secretary Dr S Jaishankar in a recent speech, adding that "when every variable is in flux, imagine the fluidity of the world." The next few years will require more of that imagination from the Modi government as it seeks to define India's position in the world where a dose of dependability may be at more of a premium than before.

I am afraid Suhasini Haidar has missed one major point. After all Narendra Modi is stereotyped in the Indian tradition of Sanatana Dharma. He is aware of the *Arthashastra* of Kautilya. It is Kautilya's unique combination of pragmatism and eternal values of Dharma that those who look only to non-Indian precedents are sure to miss. Suhasini has also fallen into this trap.

In the context of the Balochistan's policy, she speculates that there is a law of diminishing returns that accompanies unpredictability as the shock value of the government's manoeuvre wears off. She also cautions that not everyone like surprises. China and Pakistan most notably expected to counter the doctrine with an overly aggressive defence posture could then lead to more tensions and India's frontiers just when the Modi government may want to focus on economic and domestic policies on the eve of elections due in 2019.

The surgical strike by the Army on September 29, 2016 might have had the impact of surprising the Pakistanis and hence they could not immediately resort to their atomic blackmail. Let us not forget that unlike the 'nuclear brahmacharya' announced by the Government of India, Pakistan has no such compunctions and it is this nuclear blackmail, which probably kept the previous governments from go even resorting to the surgical strike of the type adopted by the Army under the clear and positive direction of the Modi government.

In this context, the fact should be appreciated that the initiatives taken by the Modi government is not only on one aspect but there is a comprehensive doctrine which I would say is based on the concept of Sanatana Dharma which is the inclusive concept of looking at the entire world as a single family. This integrated approach not only underlines the message of being friendly with all the nations and at the same time also realizes the harsh reality of power politics in the world of diplomacy.

As Dr Abdul Kalam used to say, in the world of real politics, strength respects strength. The nuclear brahmacharya type policies adopted in the last 70 years only strengthened the impression that India is a country which is good at preaching and moralizing but when it came to effective action, it fails miserably. This characteristic has been described by others as India committing the mistake of considering announcements as equal to achievements. An iron hand in a velvet glove may be a correct policy in certain circumstances. But a velvet hand in a velvet glove will be a proof of extreme weakness or extreme incompetence.

All these 70 years of our foreign policy especially when it came to Pakistan we have been following a policy of a velvet hand in a velvet glove. It is this attitude that the Modi doctrine has changed dramatically into a policy of iron hand in the velvet glove. As this is in tune with the concept of Sanatana Dharma which respects all human values and at the same time ensures that national security is not compromised, there is every chance that this will succeed.

# 8

# Eight Reasons Why the Modi Government's Strategy is the Best for Demonetisation

The demonetisation of the 1,000 and 500 rupees currency notes announced by the Prime Minister on the 8th of November 2016 is perhaps the most dramatic, bold and historic effort at big bang economic reform in the country.

As a close observer and admirer of our dynamic Prime Minister and his unique style of leadership, I list below the eight reasons why the hostile stand taken against him by his opponents are not valid.

## 1. OBJECTIONS FROM THE ECONOMICS ANGLE

A classic example is the article in *The Times of India*, dated 19th December 2016, Chennai edition, in which Professor Rajeev Gowda of IIM (Bangalore), has taken on the comments made by S Gurumurthy in response to the criticism of former Prime Minister Manmohan Singh in the Rajya Sabha highlighting the negative aspects of demonetisation. The following excerpts from that article clearly bring out how Gowda had tried to show from purely economics point of view that Gurumurthy's claim that there was no job creation during the regime of UPA is not valid:

> "Former Prime Minister Manmohan Singh penned a poignant article ('Making of a Mammoth Tragedy', *The Hindu*, December 9, 2016) warning us of the impending pitfalls of the demonetisation exercise in a response, Rashtriya Swayamsevak Sangh (RSS) ideologue S Gurumurthy wrote about the economic performance of the NDA government (1999-2004) and the UPA-I government (2004 to 2009), sidestepping the entire issue of economic and social costs of demonetisation or its benefits, if any ('Not a Tragedy but the Remedy', *The Hindu*, December 13, 2016).
>
> Gurumurthy's argument goes like this: GDP grew rapidly from 2004 to 2009. Asset prices (stock markets, gold, real estate) also grew rapidly during this period as did the share for high denomination currency notes in circulation. He then uses a misleading number for jobs generated in this period to make the point that GDP growth in this period was 'fake' growth. He then argues that huge amounts of 'black cash' led to asset price inflation which led to high GDP growth. This bizarre argument then goes on to justify how invalidating high denomination currency notes overnight was the remedy for this surfeit of 'black cash'. Gurumurthy misdiagnoses a non-existent problem for which apparently the demonetisation initiative is a remedy.
>
> India's GDP growth was indeed 50% higher in 2004 to 2009 (UPA-I) vis-a-vis 1999 to 2004 (NDA-I). Asset

> prices also rose sharply between 2004 and 2009. These are valid, independent observations in themselves and are natural correlates in most economies. This does not imply that rising asset prices were the reason for high GDP growth – correlation is not causation. Further, hard data refute the allegation that it was merely wealth effects of asset price inflation that drove GDP growth during UPA-I."

The learned argument advanced by Gowda fails when applied the simple test of whether the jobs created even in the organized sectors were long-term solutions and represented real addition to the economy. Even smugglers and drug runners, create jobs for those who are involved in the gold, gun and drug running but can any serious economist argue that job creation by any means will be justified, even if it has got negative social impact?

The series of scandals of UPA regime, like the 2G, 3G, CWG are a standing condemnation of how the so-called job creation under that regime took place. Is the job creation of that regime different from the jobs created under earlier scams like the Harshad Metha stock market scam, the vanishing companies scam and Ponzi schemes like Teak Equity? Let us not forget these scams also created jobs when they lasted.

In fact, Japan has not yet recovered from the recruit scandal of the eighties round this time was the collapse of the so-called tiger economies of the South-East Asia starting with Thailand and covering Hong Kong, Indonesia and so on.

Corporate governance became a buzzword and the movement to check corruption in public life became universal, resulting in the Anti-Corruption Convention of 2003.

The dawn of the 21st century saw the dotcom bust.

The great economic meltdown of 2008 itself was a case of financial engineering running amok, leading to the subprime crisis. The dramatic example of how unethical application of the concept of derivatives led to a great failure was when a company blessed with couple of Nobel laureates in economics collapsed in the subprime crisis.

The whole concept of Corporate governance became relevant because of the exclusive focus on the theory that the purpose of business is maximization of profit and it's the bottomline that ultimately prevails. This was the Washington consensus preached by the IMF.

What Modi is trying to do is to put in practice, the ancient Indian concept of Sanatana Dharma. Sanatana Dharma which is what Hinduism really means.

When it comes to governance, Sanatana Dharma becomes Raj Dharma and when it comes to war and diplomacy it becomes Kautilya's *Arthashastra*. And thirdly when it comes to spiritual development it is Moksha Dharma.

In short Modi is following the Sanatana Dharma in governance.

Demonetisation follows Kautilya's *Arthashastra*.

In this approach, one does not take an exclusive view or a narrow view of even economic activity without taking moral and ethical values into account.

When dealing with crooks, the approach is different from that adopted for dealing with the honest people. "*Satam pratye satam kuryat saatam pratye saat yam kuryat*," says Kautilya.

## 2. ADOPTING SECRECY AND SURPRISING OPPONENTS

The second set of criticism relates to the suddenness and secrecy surrounding the announcement of a major policy affecting practically every citizen of a vast country of 1.25 billion population and that too a modern democracy ... government of the people, by the people and for the people. Even the cabinet ministers were not allowed to leave the cabinet room till the PM had personally announced the decision on the broadcast media. The announcement took the entire nation by surprise.

It is only now that the government is trying to come to terms with the ground realities about the sufferings of the common citizen. The media are now highlighting the suffering of the common man in queues. Especially tragic has been the cases of people who are dying and waiting in the queue.

The action of the government is described as anti-people and anti-poor. In fact, the very fact that in a huge country like ours, the demonetisation has been introduced and has been implemented during the past six weeks, should be compared with the current experience of a small country like Venezuela in South America. That government wanted to demonetise their largest currency of 100 bolivar notes and they had to postpone the implementation of the policy by a few months, thanks to the strong protest and law and order problem created by the citizens immediately after announcement.

The very fact that in the country the people have by and large welcomed this measure shows the extent to which public are supporting silently the initiative of the government. As the Prime Minister rightly observed in the public meeting on 19th

December 2016 at Kanpur that the success and the credit for the demonetisation as an effort at elimination of black money and corruption will go to the 1.25 billion people of the country and not to any individual leader or the government.

## 3. INADEQUATE PLANNING AND AD HOC IMPLEMENTATION

The next point of criticism is about the lack of proper planning and ad hocism in the implementation. In fact, what is considered as lack of planning and ad hocism is in itself the strength of the current government's capacity to think on its feet and take immediate corrective action instead of being slow footed and thereby giving opportunities for the crooks to game the system and with the help of the bad apples in institutions in the Reserve Bank of India and the banking system itself launder all the black money!

The very fact that the government has been alert and has come with quick responses should be appreciated instead of criticising that government has not done enough prior thinking. In fact, among the leaders who are criticizing the PM and the government are people who are admirers of Deng Xiaoping who was able to lead the Chinese economy to the path of explosive growth after death of Mao. He explained his success by responding to changing situations and innovating 'by feeling the stones', as he said. While in the case of Deng Xiaoping, his flexibility is appreciated and the economic results are admired, when it comes to Narendra Modi who is attempting to apply the same strategy in our country, these very pundit have been complaining out how everything should have been previously thought through.

The simple idea of the whole matter is that if 86% of the money in the system is withdrawn, an equal quantity of money should be provided at least in time, but the real point is that quite a lot of this 86% varying from 20-50% according to estimates is black money used for malpractices.

This is repeatedly confirmed by the fact that in the States like UP, many villages have been reporting about how people are just waiting to help poor people permit them to deposit money in their Jan Dhan Yojana accounts. If everything was about board, this phenomenon would not have taken place. Bibek Debroy in a news channel town hall meeting confirmed that while in the southern States the complaints of the poor waiting in the queues has come down, in the Bihar, UP and West Bengal the complaints continue.

There is also criticism that demonetisation has been announced without proper preparation and educating the people about the alternatives to cash based transactions. This has been answered in details in the article of A Surya Prakash in *The New Indian Express* dated 20th December 2016 under the title 'Tune in to Mann Ki Baath':

> "This criticism may not hold if one re-visits his public utterances before November 8 and also examines the growth of black money and wealth between 2004-2014 and the consequences of continued Manmohan Singh style pussy-footing for the nation's economy.
>
> So first, the question as to whether Modi had foolishly rushed in where angels fear to tread or whether demonetisation was part of a well-thought out strategy. There were several occasions when Modi touched upon the issue of e-wallets or electronic banking prior to November 8, but there was one

occasion during which he made his intentions absolutely clear. That was on May 22 during his show on All India Radio – Mann ki Baat.

For those who listened to him that day, November 8 would have held no surprises. Obviously, Modi was mulling this option quite some time ago, because even as early as May – a full five months prior to demonetisation – he had urged people in his radio programme to move from cash to a less-cash economy when he said: "We will have to change our old habits ... the world is moving towards a cashless society ... through electronic technology ... there is no question of our wallets getting stolen.

The Pradhan Mantri Jan Dhan Yojana has ensured that almost every family came into the banking system and got a RuPay Card, which is useful both as a debit and credit card; also, with the very small instrument called Point of Sale machines now in vogue, one can make payments.

Then there is the Bank on Mobile – the Universal Payment Interface banking; and finally, there is the Aadhaar Card and the fact that practically everyone in the country has a mobile phone. There is no need to carry around any cash. Therefore, by synchronising Jan Dhan, Aadhaar and the mobile (JAM), we can move ahead towards a cashless society." He virtually prepared the minds of his listeners that day to what was coming when he said, "If we learn and adapt ourselves to use these services, then we will not require currency ... businesses will function automatically ... underhand dealings will stop, the influence of black money will be reduced.

So I appeal to my countrymen, that we should at least make a beginning. Once we start, we will move ahead with great ease." He also called upon people to overcome the fear of the unknown. He said 20 years ago who would have thought that so many people would have mobile phones. "Yet, we caught on to it and now we cannot do without cell phones. Maybe this cashless society assumes a similar form. But the sooner this happens, the better it will be," he said. Could any prime minister have been more explicit than this about his intention to launch a major assault on black money, demonetise currency and nudge the society towards a less-cash economy?"

## 4. CHECKING TERRORISM FUNDED BY ISI PROVIDING FAKE INDIAN CURRENCY TO JEHADIS

The next aspect is about the demonetisation and its impact on fighting terrorism. The suddenness with which the announcement was made has literally been a shock to the Pakistan-inspired terrorism and the fierce insistence of the security agencies that we should use only the currency notes manufactured within the note paper manufactured in our country and not use imported currency-paper prove that the object of choking the terrorists by starving them of fake currency has succeeded, because in the past currency paper was imported, it gave an easy opportunity to Pakistan to play havoc with our border areas and our economy by funding terrorists.

## 5. ATTACK ON THE LEGALITY OF THE GOVERNMENT ORDER ON DEMONETISATION

Another angle of attack on the demonetisation is from the purely legal aspect. The issue has been challenged in the court and as the matter is subjudice, we have to wait for the decision of the Supreme Court.

From the stand adopted by the judiciary so far, one can safely presume that our judiciary has set up a very healthy and high standard when it comes to interpretation of the Constitution and there have been quite a few occasions especially after the emergency when the Supreme Court has come with concepts like the 'basic structure of the Constitution' and 'defence of the fundamental rights of the citizens of the country'. The management of the economy and evolving appropriate policies is a purely executive function and we can expect that the judiciary will not interfere and take on the role of executive itself.

In the past, it is because of the delay in amendment of laws, which given the opportunity for the corrupt elements to flourish. A classic example is the Benami Transactions Prohibition Act, 1989 under which Rules were not framed till now. Every time any law exists, the crooks find ways to locate the loopholes and exploit the legal loopholes and not allowing loopholes will develop by action in real time is one of the strong points of the current government and the manner which it has gone about implementing the demonetisation scheme.

The basic source corruption in the system and the all pervasive corruption and poor governance in the country has been the corruption emanating from politics. The *neta, babu, lala, jhola, dada* syndrome has had a long run in our country and Modi government's effort at demonetisation is the first effective step taken to tackle this menace. The Election Commission has also come up with a recommendation that there should be total transparency and even funds, the current exemption to political parties should be brought down to ₹2,000. There are 1,480 political parties registered with Election Commission of which only about 400 are contesting elections and the remaining have been only on paper just to act as conduits for collection of black money. The current instructions that up to ₹20,000 can be collected without giving details is also sought to be reduced by the Election Commission to ₹2,000. Ideally there should be no exemption at all for political parties, they funds should be all transparent process and through the normal banking system. After all, other democracies have systems and there is no reason why India cannot clean up its democratic system, that too after 70 years of independence.

## 6. MODI IS FOLLOWING TRUMP, CHARISMA CANNOT BE THE BASIS OF LAW-MAKING

Mathew Idiculla in an oped article in *The Times of India*, Chennai edition, dated 16th December 2016 makes interesting comments about the personalised approach to policy making by Modi in the case of demonetisation:

> "The Centre's move rendering 86% of the currency invalid raises serious legal and institutional questions. Can the promise made by the RBI governor be rescinded by the government in such a manner? Further, can the Centre restrict a citizen's right to withdraw their own money? In this article, I examine how the demonetisation policy deinstitutionalises the state as it undermines the rule of law and instead seeks to legitimise public policy through charismatic authority. Demonetisation and the rule of law: One of the prerequisites of a State governed by the rule of

law is that legal and institutional norms are stable, clear and predictable.

Decision-making cannot be impetuous or arbitrary. But unlike previous instances of demonetisation in 1956 and 1978, the latest move by the government has come via an executive and not a legislative action. The notification for cancellation of the legal tender status of the notes (the Attorney General seeks to distinguish it from demonetisation) was issued under Section 26 (2) of the RBI Act. This provision states that the Centre can, "on recommendation of the Central Board" of RBI, declare that "any series of bank notes of any denomination shall cease to be legal tender." Hence, the government has to demonstrate with documentary evidence that the decision was indeed taken as per the advice of the RBI and not by the whims of the prime minister. There is also no clarity regarding the legal basis on which limits and conditions were placed on cash withdrawals. The RBI Act does not have any such provision.

Article 300A of the Constitution provides that right to property can only be restricted by the authority of law. Since bank notes are movable property, any restriction on its access must be provided by law. However, demonetisation was carried out without issuing an ordinance or amending any law. Further, for people without bank accounts, demonetisation amounts to compulsory acquisition of property without provision for compensation as their old currency is no longer exchangeable. Since the launch of demonetisation, there have been multiple policy somersaults which further raises legal questions. For example, while the notification clearly states that old 500 and 1,000 rupee notes can be exchanged until December 30,

> on November 24, the government abruptly declared there will no longer be any exchange. Such U-turns go against the doctrine of legitimate expectations, an essential principle of the rule of law which provides that people have a legitimate right to expect a public authority to honour a promise or policy proclamation."

A new language of legitimacy: The ad hocism in decision-making regarding demonetisation erodes the institutional legitimacy of the Indian State. The institutional crisis afflicting the country has exacerbated over the years as individual whims take precedence over institutional norms. What we are witnessing now is not just personalisation of political power but also that of public policy. The demonetisation policy was not announced by the RBI or finance ministry It came as a personal appeal by Modi. The promotion of partisan agendas can also be seen in the design of the new 500 and 2,000 rupee notes. These notes unabashedly promote Modi's pet scheme Swachh Bharat Abhiyan and, more controversially, don Devanagari numerals. It is important to note that Article 343 of the Constitution states that only the "international form of Indian numerals" shall be used for official purposes. This was the result of a delicate compromise struck by the members of the Constituent Assembly on the vexed language question.

Now this constitutional settlement is also being undone. As demonetisation continues to take a heavy toll on the common man (reportedly causing more than 90 deaths) even after a month, our ministers remind us that we are undergoing a 'cultural revolution' to replace the old order and create a 'new normal'. This new normal seems to have little regard for law, economics, historic agreements, institutional propriety or even basic humanity. Legitimacy of State action is instead based on a leader's virtue and his appeal to the inner virtue of all people.

In Narendra Modi's address to the people on November 8, he said, "In this fight against corruption, black money, fake notes and terrorism, in this movement for purifying our country, will our people not put up with difficulties for some days? I have full confidence that every citizen will stand up and participate in this mahayagna." There is a Gandhiesque call for a grand sacrifice. Even if demonetisation causes inconvenience to people, its virtue legitimises suffering. Standing in long queues is an essential rite of passage in the moral purification of our country. In the post-revolution moral republic, legitimacy is not primarily derived from the Weberian idea of rational-legal authority of the State but rather on the charismatic authority of the leader. Authority flows, not from the rule of law or the barrel of the gun, but from the leader's ability to persuade people to sacrifice. The politics of morality is the currency of charismatic authority and this further deinstitutionalises the State. For all its charisma, such a form of authority is also most tenuous for if it fails to keep the people enchanted, the revolution will relapse.

## 7. PUBLIC FUNDING OF ELECTIONS

One of the suggestions made by the reformers is public funding for elections is a better remedy than demonetisation. But in Germany, where such public funding is allowed, there was still case of fund collection beyond that and Willy Brant had to pay the price. If it can happen in a country like Germany, there is no guarantee that any public funding will be effective in our country. For the first time, Modi government's effort on demonetisation has created a genuine opportunity for cleaning up the system and that is because this government has been transparent and throughout in his career, Modi has been articulating the strategies and policies. The mistake many people made was that he was a regular run of the mill politicians for whom a cynical and hypocritical approach is taken as a norm. That is what makes all the difference and Modi is a unique leader and the current effort of demonetisation is a unique exercise in effective governance, first time since independence. The comments made earlier on the larger issue of legal cover will apply here also.

## 8. EVEN ADVANCED COUNTRIES HAVE NOT GONE TOTALLY CASHLESS, HOW CAN INDIA TRY?

The last argument is that even advanced countries like Sweden, Denmark and Japan have not gone totally cashless.

The best answer to these doubting Thomas is provided in detail by Nandan Nilekani in his book *Rebooting India*.

I am therefore very hopeful that this great unprecedented initiative of our dynamic and visionary PM Narendra Modi will succeed. In February 2017, BJP got the historic mandate of voters in four Assembly Elections – Uttar Pradesh, Uttarakhand, Goa and Manipur. It proves that people support the policies of Modi government for the development of India. We can look forward to a great India in 2017 leading the rest of the world in good governance.

# 9

# Modi as Chanakya 2017

I am a Maharashtrian Deshastha whose forefathers migrated to Tamil Nadu 300 years ago in 1676, at the time of Shivaji. We speak Marathi at home. I spent 42 years in public administration as a member of the Indian Administrative Service (IAS), Gujarat Cadre and therefore familiar with six languages – Marathi, Gujarati, Sanskrit, Tamil, English and Hindi.

With the understanding I have of the culture and the people who speak these languages, I am in a position to make an analysis of Narendra Modi as the 'Chanakya of India 2017'. I just list below my reasons for calling him the 'Chanakya of India 2017':

> Chanakya is recognized as a great pragmatic, political scientist who not only was the Dean of the famous Takshashila University, but was also the mentor of Chandragupta Maurya, who established Aryavarta, the great Magadha empire which covers a vast area from Kandahar in what is today Afghanistan and right up to Bengal with the capital at Pataliputra (modern Patna).

Chanakya, also known as Vishnu Sharma or Kautilya, had a very strong ego and a high sense of self-respect. Above all, he also an incandescent mind and had mastered the essence of Sanatana Dharma as well as all the traditional Shastras and Vedas. He was particularly a great expert in Raj Dharma, Moksha Dharma and Apat Dharma articulated by the great Vyasa in the *Mahabharata*. His magnum opus *Arthashastra* is considered to be a quintessence of wisdom of our heritage, and the Aryan civilization. Chanakya's masterpiece not only met the demands of running an effective governance which was also good governance based on the concept of ethics and justice for all.

Sanatana dharma which is articulated through *Arthashastra* of Chanakya is not only a collection principles related to ethics and morals, but also has noble ideas which are also eminently pragmatic.

The pragmatism and its effectiveness was demonstrated for all time by Chanakya who felt that the Maurya dynasty was betrayed by Nandas, by unethical means. After all, Mahananda was only the barber of Suryagupta, the Magadha emperor and the father of Chandragupta.

Mahananda murdered the emperor who trusted him and usurped his kingdom, Chandragupta was imprisoned and had no future. It was Chanakya who as the Dean of the Takshashila, strongly felt that justice has to be done. His anger was provoked by the insult he faced in the court of Mahananda. Combining his personal feelings with the political vision, he became the mentor of Chandragupta, who was likely to end up as the Indian version of the famous prince of Denmark, Hamle trapped into analysis paralysis. He made him realize the ambition of re-establishing and building a much bigger empire, the great Magadha empire.

It was Kautilya or Chanakya or Vishnu Sharma, who guided the prince at every step of the way, to use a masterly combination of Sama, Dama, Bheda and Danda leading to ultimate success.

At every step of the way, he helped Chandragupta. Basic strategies he adopted has been described as four – Sama, Dama, Bheda and Danda. Sama means marshalling arguments and persuading one to agree. Dama represents strengthening the persuasion not only with the strong logical arguments but with tempting gifts or bribes. Today, what the corrupt corporate houses are doing may be a very vigorous version of bribing or lobbying which is invoking the concept of Dama. Bheda was the next strategy with the emphasis on creating and exploiting differences or the well-known concept of divide and rule.

And finally, Danda, which is actual punishment which may in the form of building an empire involve declaring war and defeating enemy in the war. In fact, when we see the history of many corporate houses which have come up after our country became independent in 1947, we find that the business itself has become similar to war and all the Sama, Dama, Bheda and Danda tactics have been adopted by the different corporate houses at different levels.

My purpose in this chapter is to compare Narendra Modi as a leader of the nation cast in the mould of Chandragupta Maurya, who has assimilated the lessons of Chanakya thoroughly and is thus a unique phenomenon. I have chosen the label Chanakya because it is ultimately the ideas and vision that are long-lasting. Historical parallels help only to some extent. The secret of success lies in shaping old strategies to new situations.

Modi happens to be a leader of democratic India which has got a Constitution which is rightly celebrated as perhaps the longest and the most comprehensive Constitution in the world. The Constitution we have adopted in 1950 is now more than 60 years old and by the time Modi completes his first term in 2019, it would have entered its 70th year.

On the eve of the Budget for 2017, two issues were dominant on the financial scene of India. One was demonetisation and the other was Goods and Services Tax (GST). The way Narendra Modi has gone about implementing the demonetisation at every step, shows how he internalized the strategy of Chanakya. I had explained this in chapter 8 'Eight Reasons Why the Modi Government's Strategy is the Best for Demonetisation'.

I will now list ten points which I have noticed from the time he became Prime Minister in May 2014 till now to relate how every step he has taken reminds me very strongly of the fact that if Chandragupta Maurya was the disciple of Chanakya in the 3rd century BC, Narendra Modi is the twenty-first century version of Chanakya.

There were two earlier attempts of demonetisation. The first was in 1946 when Chintaman Dwarakanath Deshmukh was Governor of the Reserve Bank and RK Shanmukham Chetty was the Finance Minister and Jawaharlal Nehru was the Prime Minister. Chintaman Deshmukh was not in favour of demonetisation, Nehru and RK Shanmukham Chetty were in favour to implement the demonetisation, mainly as a means to curb the rampant black market which involved the use of high denomination currency notes like more than ₹1,000. The percentage of such high denomination notes in the currency in circulation was hardly more than 2%. The effort failed because there were some rumours about GD Naidu getting the benefits because of insider leakage in Coimbatore. Shanmukham Chetty had to resign.

The second attempt was in 1978 when Prime Minister Morarji Desai, the martinet and a strong disciplinarian, a person who was very firm in his views resorted to demonetisation of currency notes above ₹1,000, IG Patel who was the Governor of RBI did not agree. The entire effort ended in a failure.

So there has been general perception that demonetisation has not been a success in India. The conventional wisdom among the macro economist and financial experts in public finance was that demonetisation has been tried as a desperate method in many countries with poor financial discipline like South American totalitarian regimes and regimes in Africa and elsewhere.

The details which are now being released in briefing by the Ministry of Finance to the Economic Survey in the context of the budget 2017-18, it appears that demonetisation, by and large, has been successful and as it is readily considered, it might have caused some short-term gain but there is a hope that there will be long-term benefits. At least, the least charitable interpretation of this effort is that it has not been a failure but perhaps, it turned out to be a super success. How was it achieved? Modi at every stage adopted the Chanakya strategy.

**Absolute Secrecy:** There was absolute secrecy about the decision to be taken and only three or four people in the government had any idea about demonetisation in the offing. From the reports we have seen in the press, it appears that apart from the Prime Minister himself, the others who were privy to the decision were the long-term confidant and advisor to the PM, from the days as Chief Minister of Gujarat, Hasmukh Adhia (IAS officer of Gujarat Cadre, hailing from Gujarat), Urjit Patel (the hand-picked RBI Governor) and Mr R Gandhi, the real Gandhian from Pudukottai, who were sworn to secrecy of the entire initiative to be taken. The criticism was initially about the secrecy but as the days proceeded it focused on a whole range of issues which are discussed by me in chapter 8 'Eight Reasons Why the Modi Government's Strategy is the Best for Demonetisation'.

After this chapter was written, there were further developments. The Standing Committee on Finance in the Lok Sabha invited the Reserve Bank Governor to appear before it to explain the background and the issues arising out of the demonetisation. Based on the evidence, there were criticism that the autonomy of the RBI has been compromised. In fact, this criticism is not valid and Narender Pani in his article had given reasons why these points raised about autonomy of Reserve Bank. I am mentioning it particularly so that when a comprehensive view of the entire demonetisation is taken, this aspect about the so-called compromising of the RBI autonomy is seen in proper perspective.

Even after that one issue was raised about possible conflict with the Election Commission. As the demonetisation exercise was going on and the Reserve Bank was issuing guidelines about remonetisation, the Election Commission has announced polling dates for five States – Uttar Pradesh, Punjab, Uttarakhand, Manipur and Goa. But the Election Commission wanted that the ceiling should be doubled from 24,000 to more for political parties and from the reports dated 29th/30th January 2017, it appears that both the Constitutional institutions – the Election Commission and the Reserve Bank – were on a collision course. But it has been neatly resolved. In fact the Modi government had two options. They could have stuck to the stand that the RBI is not only a Statutory body and its responsibility was backed by the solid power of the legislation. Whereas, in the case of Election Commission, these powers were only for a limited period. So on the question of micro management of currency, the issue would have ultimately gone to the Supreme Court for a final decision between the power of the RBI and the legal authority for currency management, the guidelines of the Election Commission for free and fair elections would prevail. But this would have had a negative political consequence of the Modi government being painted as been not respecting tradition and trying to saffronise the entire administration. It has been neatly avoided by the Reserve Bank by taking a technical stand that while they may not relax on the issue of ATM limits, on the current accounts, limits are all removed from 1st February 2017. In other words, Modi is practising another key message of Chanakya in *Arthashastra*. It is never a good strategy to corner an enemy and leave him no escape route. After all, face is important. In the so-called Asian values, which are the subject of management debates in the 80s, when before the collapse of the South-East Asian tigers in the 1990s and scam, where as saving face guides many of the management decisions. Even in corporate matters, in China, India, Japan and Asian countries, whereas in western tradition, there is no tradition and no such aspect of saving face. I think by the way of compromising to see that other parties also lives by the sense of dignity and not totally cornered and rendered important.

In our tradition, Krishna is called Poorna Purushottam and Rama is called Maryada Purushottam. *Ramayana* becomes extremely relevant in the context of governance. Rama Rajya is still held to be the ideal for good governance and anybody familiar with the *Valmiki Ramayana* and the other classic Indian versions in every part of the country would appreciate the fact that Rama after defeating Ravana in the war gives him maximum opportunity to correct himself and kills him only when he has failed to utilize the many opportunities he has given, by Rama to come to this part of Dharma. Again in the case of Duryodhana, in *Mahabharata*, demons that I know what is the power of Dharma and what is not, but I am not able to give up Adharma and come to the part of Dharma. *Najami dharmam nathavo praharthihi najami papam nachava niverthihi.*

The RBI directive for removing the limits in the current accounts is in the spirit of the same *Ramayana* where the Ravana (in this case the black money holders) are given opportunity to come to the path of the right. The income declaration scheme which the Modi government has announced earlier is in keeping with the spirit of *Ramayana*.

Another example of the Chanakya tactics in full display we have witnessed in the case of introduction of GST. This indeed is going to be a monumental achievement in the financial management of the country which is probably long overdue and the quest for GST has almost become the quest for the holy grail. But Modi government has been able to really make a breakthrough by adopting Chanakya tactics again. In this case, the strategy of using money bill for saving the basic elements of the GST Act had only leave the other parties fuming and complaining impotently about not being given a fair treatment. But, at the end of the day, it is the proof of pudding is in the eating. It is when we examine the political dimension of demonetisation that we can appreciate the Chanakya elements of Modi government strategy more clearly by the timing of the demonetisation practically all the other opposition parties have been rendered ineffective. While each one of the parties may have its own core supporters who may still supporting the parties, bulk of them have depended on money power if not muscle power for their hold in their respective areas. This has become a case where they can express their frustration, they were not able to reverse the process of demonetisation. Because, ultimately, it is the final results which matters when the drips are down. On the other hand, while the BJP and the RSS are being accused of being majoritarian, they have not been able to be effective for bulk of their existence because, the majority did not effectively materialize. It was only in the 2014 elections the majority was welded with solid core which seem to ensure longevity at least in the medium term. Institutions like Art of Living and Baba Ramdev's organization have become solid supporters of the BJP and that is apart from the traditional supporters of the party. Today have reached levels perhaps of 35-40% can guarantee its longevity. At the moment the other second activity at which the Modi government is focusing attention is spreading the footprints of the BJP in States where it had no presence all these years of its existence. The skilful utilization of the local conditions and the strategic alliances with local parties and seizing power have been demonstrated for example in Assam and Haryana.

Glimpses of the Chanakyan thinking are visible if we examine practically every decision on appointment of key personnel done by the Modi government since it is in power. Governors play a major role especially when influencing the state of State politics are concerned and in this the BJP has been particularly focusing. A record is mixed because, sometimes they have been too clever by harm and appointment of Governors who were exclusively from the BJP's table had lead to even constitutional embarrassment and displeasure of the Supreme Court and the judiciary. Perhaps, Arunachal Pradesh and Uttarakhand are cases in point. Nevertheless, some of these appointments have turned to be very astute like the appointment of former Chief Justice of India as the Governor of Kerala. In the recent Jallikattu explosion which has very serious consequences especially on the federal structure and operation of co-operative federalism, this particular individual who has the deeper understanding of the culture of Tamil Nadu has made a valuable contribution by ensuring that the legal plays through which the Jallikattu had to be piloted especially with the opposition of the activists under the animal rights and the Provision of Cruelty to Animal Act as well as environmentalists have indeed been very valuable. In fact, the instant introduction of the legislation for long-term performance and observance of Jallikattu has been greatly aided by very critical and insightful inputs given by the Governor of Tamil Nadu. This is what we learn from the newspaper reports like *The Indian Express* of 31st January 2017.

The across the board wide spectrum steps of ensuring a 'Congress Mukt Bharat' involve that the Narendra Modi government has kept the overall objective in the mind and never for a moment, whether it is a major step or a minor step, lost sight of the objective. And it is this focus which invokes the *Kathopanishad* invocation – *Uttishthatada jaggruta propthuvara nibhodita*.

The further confirmation of this I got from the budget discussion that was aired by NDTV on 1st February 2017 soon after the Budget was released in the afternoon of 1st February 2017. Keity Mistry pointed out that while this is a very sensible budget and the decision about handling fiscal deficit as well as the budget deficit have been treated in a professional manner and perhaps the demonetisation and the secrecy that went around it which itself was a point of criticism of many others about the autonomy of the RBI being compromised has resulted in ultimately a fact that elections are taking place did not influence the overall phase of managing the fiscal deposit and the budgetary deposit. The demand made for postponing the budget after the elections on 11th March 2017 was on the basis that the budget will be used as tool for influencing the votes with freebies and so on. That could be avoided because of the professional secrecy maintained by the four people who according to the Press were the people in the know of the timing of the demonetisation decision, the Prime Minister himself, the RBI Governor, Hasmukh Adhia, IAS and the Deputy Governor of RBI, R Gandhi.

The critics have been silenced by the delicate balancing of different vested interests like opposition parties cunning the government on political front and the financial experts looking for an opportunity to criticize the government for using the Budget for buying votes and influencing the overall directives of the Election Commission about the Code of Conduct for the polls. It is a triple success achieved, because the Modi government adopted the principles of Raja Dharma and the *Arthashastra* as codified by Chanakya.

The delicate balance between the subsidies and the canibdies of budget deficit has been neatly achieved because of following the principles of Chanakya in the Budget of 2017. In fact, the challenge before the Finance Minister was more than that of Ulysses, because Ulysses had to manage between two dangers whereas the Finance Minister had to balance between these two and also a third factor called the current account liability or the requirement under the Responsible Budget Deficit Act to which government is legally committed. Instead of following steady glide path of the Chief Economic Advisor of 2%, NK Singh Committee has recommended 3.5% and he stuck a balance of 2.5% for 2017-18, thereby the same goal of controlling current account liability, after all visualized under the Responsible Budget Deficit Act 2013 could be achieved by 2020. This acrobatic balancing on the financial front would not have been possible but for the Chanakya principle adopted by the Modi government.

In fact, the resources required for more effective implementation of development of employment schemes like MNREGA (Mahatma Gandhi National Rural Employment Generation Act) and the higher education, progress has been made towards them also because of the Chanakya principles.

*The Economic Times*, dated 3rd February 2017, editorially commented that on the budget, arbitrarily, coercive power by taxmen. Government must guard against a taxmen raj. The rationale and the arguments articulated in the editorial which are below:

> "The component of tax revenue slated to go up the most is personal income tax. Annexure III to the Budget speech lists out a number of strong-arm measures that would presumably help the government achieve this goal. To prevent a backlash that would further discourage investment, the government must ensure that taxmen use their new powers with oversight and according to due process, and that their actions would be amenable to swift redress, should the need arise.
>
> The Budget has proposed sweeping powers for taxmen to attach property, conduct searches, call for documents and determine fair market value of assets. This goes against the tenet of a non-adversarial tax regime, leading to uncertainty for individuals and businesses. Empowering tax officers to provisionally attach properties in search cases could coerce people into making declarations, before taking legal recourse. And that is unfair. Similarly, empowering junior officers to conduct inquiries and expanding the scope of searches to cover any activity done for a charitable purpose could mean roving inquiries. Tax officers will not be obliged either to disclose reasons for a search to an appellate tribunal, to maintain confidentiality. However, search and seizures are blunt, archaic tools of law enforcement, and bring back memories of a bad pre-reform past. Instead, the need is for intelligent data mining to create tax demands and with a solid proof of evasion and avoidance."

The argument looks very perfect but these are the types of arguments that are generally advanced by a very highly intelligent authorities and experts in the area of any subjects, particularly economics. Having been an administrator but not a tax authority in my life, I have also witnessed honest exemplary officer like MR Sivaraman, IAS (1961 batch, Madhya Pradesh Cadre) who hailed highly responsible position in the Customs and Excise Departments and was the Secretary, Revenue during the NDA regime. It is not only the top level officers, but there are excellent officers in the Income Tax department at the junior level and right down to the lowest one, who many a time are witnesses and harassed. I do not want to take names, but unfortunately, the revenue administration has acquired a bad name to the extent that everybody is considered corrupt till proved their innocent. On the other hand, the reality is the department contain excellent officers who are honest at all levels. And if as in the present Modi government, there is seriousness of intent right from the Prime Minister, the Finance Minister and senior Ministers to fight corruption as the experience with the demonetisation shows, we can be reasonable that even if the congenitally corrupt junior officers resort to misuse of their powers for sheer harassment or the raidraj, they also know that they will also be pulled up. Not only that if they really accumulate the illegal wealth, they themselves will become victims of the amended laws. If any proof is needed, just look at the actions initiated against the officials of the RBI and some of the nationalized banks during the first two months of demonetisation when the complaints were received about 70 crore of new currency of 2,000 rupee notes being hijacked by clever gang of corrupt officials in the RBI and nationalized banks. *The New Indian Express* came with the expose in its January 2017 issue.

What is my reply to the very highly coherent and inherently consistent and perfect solution recommended in the Editorial of *The Economic Times*? My simple answer would be, we have not yet invented the technique for making omelette without breaking eggs.

# 10

# Epilogue

The tectonic shift to the Right in the governance of India, introduced by Narendra Modi after the elections of 2014 is still a work in progress. I have tried to articulate the significant features of this shift especially in terms of the contents of the ideology and also point out that the programme of action for good governance which has been articulated by the Modi government is indeed a pragmatic one and has many positive features. Above all it is eminently implementable.

The first two parts of this book trace the history of the development of the soul of Indian culture which I would call as Sanatana Dharma and the ideology for governance and politics based on this as the ideology for India's political right. For coming to this description I have broadly gone by all the features which any student of political science may observe. If we look at the political party system in democracies or in any other form of governance, we will find some common features. All political parties to the right generally have not only an economic dimension but also social and cultural aspects which are linked with the people of that country or place. The right of centre parties generally has a close link with the cultural, linguistic, religious, economic, political and social dimension, the left or the non-right parties generally do not claim any close link with the history, culture, religion and ethical aspects of life. Their main focus is economic and the role of the State.

The uniqueness of Sanatana Dharma and its close identity with our country, what we can call Bharatavarsha has been highlighted and in shaping this ideology, I see from the historical perspective.

Narendra Modi heading the BJP as an active politician and Mohan Bhagwat heading the RSS as a son of the Bharatmata rooted in the culture of our motherland have formed an excellent alliance. What impact this alliance can have has already been proved in the 2014 elections and will it have the impact such pairs had in the past?

That is an interesting question.

In the past, the fact that while the impact of such alliances lasted, it brought prosperity, glory, happiness and good governance in the country. In the Indian context, some of the strategic partnerships between the man of tradition and culture and the man of active politics are the following:

(i) Chanakya and Chandragupta Maurya.

(ii) Vidyaranya, Harihara and Bukka or the Yadava princes setting up the Vijayanagara empire.

(iii) Samartha Ramdas and Shivaji.

(iv) Ramakrishna Paramahamsa and Vivekananda.

The partnerships ensure that each person brings his own contribution and strength and together they become a winning combination. The question arises if the Modi government is work in progress, of Narendra Modi and Mohan Bhagwat, what is the future likely to be.

The effective articulation and communication of how Sanatana Dharma is different from the traditional way of looking at Hinduism. Perhaps in our country, no other organization has been subjected to such systematic, continuous, hostile misinterpretation as the RSS, ever since it was founded 80 years ago. Then 2014 election has provided an opportunity for not only reinventing the RSS but also introduce in the effective governance of the country, the principles of the soul of Sanatana Dharma which will provide the basis for the long time sustenance of good governance and prosperity of the country.

The task is all the more challenging because the new philosophy has to be articulated along with running the challenge of governing a vast country like India which has the second largest population in the world.

While propagating what is new and unique about the reinvented RSS, the philosophy of the BJP has also to be clearly articulated. There was once a stage where the RSS was very much focused on Swadeshi that organizations like Swadeshi Jagran Manch advocated approaches to issues like globalization from a totally hostile point of view. BJP under Narendra Modi gladly welcomes NRIs who represent the enterprising global spirit of Indians today.

The very fact that throughout his campaign, Modi has been talking about globalization and the role of India in the modern comity of nations and India as a global economic power shows that he is Swadeshi at heart but he realizes that a Swadeshi of the 21st century of India has to be different from those who were Indians in the colonial period. If the RSS does not change with time, it will not be able to provide the healthy systems needed for the governance of modern 21st century India.

At the same time, the positive dimensions of the RSS and the BJP based on the philosophy of the Sanatana Dharma should be highlighted –

(i) there will always be the ethical dimension,

(ii) there will be an inclusive approach ensuring prosperity for all,

(iii) there will be justice in every aspect of life, and

(iv) the values of Sanatana Dharma will motivate every person not only to become excellence insofar as skill development is concerned and at the same time, also become a professional by not sacrificing the ethical dimension for clear monitory or selfish claims.

Perhaps most significant aspect of Sanatana Dharma is the love for the motherland. Hence, the safety and national security becomes supremely important and the capacity to develop defence technologies and defend ourselves and not become the largest importer of weapons is the sad result of the 70 years of the left of centre governance can be corrected.

When it comes to a project like Namami Gange, it is possible to use the love of Ganga and inspiration of Sanatana Dharma as the spring board for bring about dramatic environmental changes for the better and ensure that Ganga is not only Nirmal but also Aviral.

What about the future? It is said that it is difficult to

predict anything especially the future. But one point is clear. Narendra Modi and Mohan Bhagwat together have already proved that it is possible to achieve the political miracle in India by using the same democratic system and come to a position of power to guide the governance of the country for five years from 2014 to 2019.

Will the right of centre government will be able to continue in the future? Will it have the lasting impact in the politics of the country? That depends on a number of factors. But this much is certain. The people of India have been given an opportunity to look at a totally coherent, more valuable and better approach to the governance of the country which not only provides solutions on the material side but also on the non-material side, including culture, religion and social harmony.

As we see the so-called left 'secular' identity-based ideologies of social or caste justice have only increased the element of selfishness, mutual hatred, suspicion and hostility in the society. Even if the Modi government is not able to come to power in the future, at least it has already shown that there is a possibility of ideal governance in our country drawing inspiration from the very roots of the soul of our Bharatmata. This development in itself will warm and gladden the heart of every true patriotic Indian.

# APPENDICES

## Appendix 1

# Out of Frauds Comes Development: Modi Government's Formula for Development

In his famous political satire on communism in *Animal Farm*, George Orwell made the legendary comment, "All animals are equal, but some animals are more equal than others." Modi government blasting into the third year of its term, seems to have derived inspiration from this comment for a totally different, but very positive impact on good governance and national development.

How? Read on.

Everybody knows that the UPA governments I and II which ruled the country from 2004 to 2014 set a long shameful track record of financial frauds and scams, one after the other. Each case was trying to beat in brazenness and size, the record of its predecessor.

These scams however have had the impact of not only highlighting the weaknesses in our system of financial architecture of business but also the loop holes that were being exploited. One positive impact has been the realization that there should be greater transparency in the corporate sector to reduce the scope for underhand dealings. After all sun light is the best antidote for disinfection.

Secondly, and more importantly, the scams highlighted the fact, that the winding up of enterprises that failed should be made easier. Under the leftist socialist approach, saving the jobs in the organised sector had become paramount. The Bureau of Industrial and Financial Reconstruction (BIFR) had become so slow in its operations that it was derisively called the Bureau of Industrial Funeral Rights! Unlike The US accepting failure of an enterprise had a lot of shame. This discouraged the setting up of new enterprises.

The *Bible* says out of evil cometh good. These frauds, each treated in a different way, are one more example of that biblical statement. In a way, they provided an opportunity for Narendra Modi and the BJP to bring about a regime change and provide good governance for the country.

Three frauds on a grand scale had grabbed the attention of the national media in recent years. They are the Satyam scam, the Sahara scam and the Kingfisher scam. Some financial frauds are more equal than others. This comes out clearly when we recall how each was handled by the players concerned.

Let us begin with the Satyam scam of 2009. Here was an iconic company in the sunrise sector of Information Technology which had become part of the legendary SWITCH (Satyam, Wipro, Infosys, TCS, Cognizant and HCL) companies. It had become one of the largest employers engaging 52,000 people and a business turnover of hundreds of crores. It had a very distinguished Board of Directors including professors from Harvard, teaching corporate governance and senior ex-bureaucrats like the retired Cabinet Secretary. Nevertheless till Ramalinga Raju, the entrepreneur behind the entire enterprise himself confessed in a 7 page letter in January 2009 that the profits in the accounts of the company had been window dressed for seven years, no one suspected any wrongdoing. To add to the embarrassment the Institute of Directors had honoured the company by awarding the Golden Peacock Award for the year 2008.

The manner in which this case of fraud was handled was unique. Ramalinga Raju was virtually protected by the State police taking on the investigation and him in custody inspite of the keenness of the Central Government agencies like CBI and regulators like SEBI to look into the scam. The government was anxious not to lose credibility and above all save the jobs of the 52,000 people who were employed by Satyam. The Government of India took the initiative to appoint a board of highly competent, professional people of unimpeachable integrity including Deepak Parekh, Kiran Karnik etc. In 100 days the board arranged to ensure that the company management was restructured and a reputed company like Mahindra and Mahindra Limited (M&M) took over Satyam.

This was a remarkable case where the government ensured that the fraud did not result in the destruction of an iconic company. But at the same time Ramalinga Raju himself and others connected with the fraud received the punishment under the law.

The impact of Satyam scam on the issue of corporate governance provided an excellent opportunity to Narendra Modi to mobilise public opinion and make the clear electoral promise that there would be no corruption in Modi government. It is to the credit of Modi government that there has been not even a whisper of the UPA type scams since it took over the governance of the country in 2014.

The second fraud of the UPA era is Sahara scam where Subroto Roy built-up a massive enterprise on a totally different concept of a large number of people coming together and pooling their resources. The strong political links Subroto Roy had, helped him on the way but when the bubble burst he still evaded arrest for a long time. He had been directed by the court to raise crores of rupees for being let off on bail and the drama is still continuing. In this case also a large number of people of the middle class had been victimized but the results are not yet clear. Modi government, after coming to power has followed the case closely to ensure that Subroto Roy faces the full brunt of the court's orders and does not enjoy clandestine support from the government.

One sure-fire antidote to fraud is transparency. The main focus of the Modi government is on achieving this goal. In fact, the enormous importance given to digital technology is to build transparency across the entire spectrum of government. The PM has never hesitated to make dramatic U-turns in policy in the interests of good governance. The decisions on Aadhaar and GST are the most important ones.

The latest in the frauds has been that of Kingfisher and the shenanigans of Vijay Mallya who seems to have launched airlines running into losses of crores of rupees. His lifestyle and the suspected collusion of influential people in the financial sector and politics has become a test case of whether the laws will operate upholding the principle of equality before law for the common citizens and the super rich.

While the Mallya case has many dimensions, the most important is the issue of ease of doing business. In the long run no government can afford to create jobs for every citizen. This will come only from the enterprising animal spirits of the people. Initiatives like 'Make in India' and encouraging strat-ups call for removing the hassles of winding up failed enterprises. The legislative measures for amending laws relating to bankruptcy and providing venture capital are most important Modi government measures taken in this context.

It is a cliche to say that failures are stepping stones for success. This calls for learning from failures and initiating corrective measures. At the national level this calls for vision and humility to learn, Modi government has given ample proof of its pragmatic vision and wisdom in its tenure so far.

We can look forward to a better future.

## Appendix 2

# BJP 2016: Inventing a New Brand

S Gurumurthy, one of the most insightful political commentators, has explained his take on the recently concluded 2016 elections in five States. In his article entitled 'Pre-Independence Congress Reincarnates as Expanding BJP' published in *The New Indian Express* dated 21st May 2016, he observes –

> "The headlines of the just concluded Assembly elections in the four States from the north-east corner to southern most India is this: Congress continues to contract in its traditional strongholds and the BJP is continuously expanding to fill the gap.... Why this shift away from the grand old party which inherited the power and prestige of the national movement for freedom.... In the name of fake secularism it disowned all that its forefathers had held dear in pre-Independence days – the ideal of Rama Rajya held out by Mahatma Gandhi, the lofty spiritual nationalism expounded by Swami Vivekananda, the spirit of Bankim Chandra's 'Vande Mataram' and the high ideal of Sanatana Dharma that Maharishi Aurobindo equated to Indian nationalism – these profound thoughts, not the fake secularism now dominating the political discourse inspired the people to sacrifice for the nation's freedom."

Gurumurthy goes on to advise that this shift calls for more than electoral and statistical analysis to understand its depth. Now the BJP needs to convince the people of India that its philosophy and programme wholly align with the spirit and icons of the freedom movement which the Congress has discarded. The BJP needs to use the idioms of the freedom movement to re-articulate its position.

If there is one very important point which Narendra Modi and the BJP led by him have repeatedly proved in the last decade, it is that they have mastered the art of the modern digital media and use it to the hilt to win elections decisively. Some of the techniques like holographic projections which Modi used in the 2014 elections, I am sure, shocked the complacent Congress-led UPA into a defeat. They are still in a mode of denial and have yet to come to terms with the changed realities. Gurumurthy's sound advice means that BJP 2016 needs a new brand for its political ideology.

As I see it, ironically the new brand has to have an ancient name – Sanatana Dharma. It is not only with Aurobindo that the expression is connected but practically with all seers and reformers of the Hindu religion.

The name Hindu itself was given by outsiders to describe our way of life which is Sanatana Dharma. This in turn has led to a lot of misunderstanding and criticism. The left of centre and secular writers never tire of making Hinduism, Hindutva as a punching bag for venting their spleen.

There are many writers who still characterize BJP as promoting Hindutva. The definition of Hindutva as given by Veer Savarkar has a militant or muscular connotation and is the basis of the label Saffron Terror used by the critics of BJP and RSS.

Using a specific term like Sanatana Dharma will ensure that we do not fall into a type of conceptual or linguistic trap into which, apocryphally, a serious minded, thorough going German-Shakespearean scholar is set to have been caught. He did a lot of research and published his finding as follows: The plays of William Shakespeare were not written by him but by another person of the same name.

Apart from escaping the linguistic trap, the following core principles of Sanatana Dharma make it an evergreen and relevant political philosophy which will ensure against the boiled frog syndrome.

- The concepts of Shanti mantra like *matrudevo bhava, pitrudevo bhava, acharyadevo bhava, atithidevo bhava*.
- The Vedantic principle *atmano mokshartham jagat hitaya cha* (at the individual level strive for release from the circle of birth and death. So long as you are alive be helpful to others and work for the welfare of the community).
- *Vasudhaiva kutumbakam* (the whole world is one family).
- *Aano bhadra krtavo yantu vishwatah* (let noble thoughts come to us from every side – Rigveda).

# Appendix 3

# Is Modi Government the Best Model of Democratic Leadership in Independent India?

India is in its 70th year of Independence. In these seven decades we have witnessed different models of democratic leadership.

Abraham Lincoln defined democracy as government of the people, by the people and for the people.

The current series of direct action by civil society activists started with Anna Hazare's movement in 2010 for the Jan Lokpal. Arvind Kejriwal, who was his associate in that popular media savvy campaign, parted ways with the Gandhian style of Anna and launched his own political party – Aam Aadmi Party (AAP). AAP was a new star in politics, in the beginning, focused attention on the single issue of corruption in public life.

Simultaneously, it also raised the issue of the type of democracy we have in our country. Are our leaders democratic? Are they in touch with the citizens, their needs, problems and aspirations? Do our MPs and MLAs reflect the will of the people?

Arvind Kejriwal represented the angst of the urban educated middle class, who had had enough of the cynical amoral stye of the political leaders of today. They were sick of the culture of corruption. India against corruption was the single focus and theme of their campaign. Hailing from the middle class which was voluble in complaining against netas, but always fought shy of entering the rough and tumble of politics, AK rushed where angels had feared to tread so far. And AAP was the result.

AAP is also a champion of direct democracy. Referendums are the instruments of direct democracy. The BREXIT Referendum of 23rd June 2016 has given a boost and made DD (Direct Democracy) a live issue.

Is referendum the best way of direct good democratic governance?

Unfortunately the only country with a long experience in such referendums is Switzerland. In the United States, California is the bell weather State, open to new ideas. This State perhaps has had the maximum cases of referendums on various local issues, including the recall of governors who fail to perform. Nevertheless their overall experience in terms of delivering good governance does not appear to be very happy.

In the ultimate analysis, democracy as represented by the will of the people reflected through the candidates elected by the voters seems to have had a much longer and better track record. Winston Churchill summed it up best and was absolutely right when he observed that democracy may be the worst form of government but all other forms of government seem to be worse.

In India, at the time of independence we adopted the British pattern of parliamentary democracy almost as a natural development. It seems to have worked in a robust manner for these seven decades.

This achievement and unique track record of our country is also largely thanks to some of our robust institutions of India like the judiciary especially the Supreme Court, the Election Commission of India and the Comptroller and Auditor General of India. These have emerged as highly credible independent institutions which play their role in ensuring that the checks and balances visualized in the Constitution are implemented in practice.

The three pillars of our governance are the legislature which make the law, the judiciary which interpret the law and the executive, including both the permanent bureaucracy and the elected members of the legislature, which implements the law. The smooth functioning of governance is supplemented and ensured by the specific agencies like the free media and civil society organisations (a whole tribe of NGOs) along with institutions like CVC and Commission for RTI play an active role in the democratic process.

While we can be happy with the track record of independent India so far, it will be worth examining which prime minister or government displayed the best model of democratic leadership.

The Prime Minister is the head of the government and we have had 11 PMs so far. The challenges and the issues they faced were vastly different. It may be invidious to compare and rate them. Nevertheless such an exercise may yield valuable insights to a student of political science.

I would suggest that we can use two vital tests to rate the different models of political leadership displayed so far by our prime ministers.

The first test is good governance and the second test is internal transparency and democratic functioning of political parties. After all it is the political parties that mobilise public opinion on issues in a real democracy.

This second test is necessary to ensure that meritocracy prevails in politics when it comes to political leadership. This will avoid the consequential dangers of dynasty and identity politics. These defects have become the common features of most of the political parties in our country today.

Before we proceed further let us be clear about the first test of good governance. As I see it good governance would mean the following:

- Rule of Law.
- Minimum corruption.
- Providing an environment where every citizen can rise to his full human potential.
- Maximum total factor productivity. (This means that there should be no wastage of any resource including human resources, physical and financial resources as well as time. Red tape and delays in governance are breeding grounds of corruption and failure to deliver public goods like health, education and national security.)

The 11 Prime Ministers who have held the office since independence so far have left us broadly with four types of political leadership models.

The first type is the pure democratic model inspired by the British Parliament with a history of seven hundred years. This was natural, as we were a British colony. The other democratic model is the United States, which is more than two hundred years old. The US itself was a British colony to begin with.

Jawaharlal Nehru and Lal Bahadur Shastri our first two prime ministers performed the great and vital function of presiding over the welding of our huge country into a single modern nation and making it into the largest functioning democracy in the world. They built vital institutions like the Election Commission and a free press which gave a voice to our young democracy. Lal Bahadur Shastri showed great moral courage and leadership and integrity in public life unmatched by any of his successors so far, till Narendra Modi formed his government in 2014. He highlighted the role of the Jawan and Kisan in our country (recall Lal Bahadur Shastri's famous slogan 'Jai Jawan Jai Kisan'). He laid the foundation for the green and white revolutions.

Unfortunately these leaders could not check the growth of regionalism and fissiparous tendencies thanks to the linguistic re-organization of States in 1956 and the anti-Hindi agitation in Tamil Nadu (the State of Madras as it was called at that time) in 1965. Jammu and Kashmir became a long-running problem from 1944 itself thanks to the policies of Nehru.

The second type of a strong political leadership was ushered by our third Prime Minister Indira Gandhi. She held office in two spells for fifteen years The first spell of eleven years 1960 to 1977 saw many positive developments like the green revolution, the white (milk) revolution and the blue one of peaceful nuclear explosion in 1974.

Unfortunately her tenure was marred by major negative developments like the erosion of institutions (like the bureaucracy). The imposition of Emergency in 1975 was a break in the saga of India's democracy. Ironically, it left the nation stronger as a democracy in 1977. After all it was the inherent fundamental urge of Indira Gandhi herself to seek democratic legitimacy which led her to call for the general elections of 1977. It is very important to remember that she could have chosen the path of dictatorship, like many other contemporary leaders of her generation. It is to her eternal credit that she chose the option of democracy.

One sad legacy of Indira Gandhi was that the Indian National Congress became totally dependent on the Nehru Gandhi Dynasty. In view of this development she fails the second test of inner party democracy. Her political leadership fails the test of good democratic leadership.

That brings us to the third model of political leadership displayed by the non-Congress Prime Ministers – Morarji Desai, Charan Singh, HD Deve Gowda, Inder Kumar Gujral and Chandra Shekhar. These governments were coalitions dominated by regional parties and parties based on caste and communities. Dynastic rule, lack of transparency and corruption were common features.

PV Narasimha Rao, who was the Prime Minister hailing from the Congress party needs to be classified as an unique leader of democracy. Vinay Sitapati's masterly biography of PVN *Half Lion: How PV Narasimha Rao Transformed India* published in 2016 coinciding with the silver jubilee of the 1991 economic reforms brings out the great debt of gratitude this narration owes to him.

Modi government which came to power in 2014 represents a fourth type of political leadership. Firmly rooted in the culture and tradition of India and determined to provide development through good governance, this appears to me to be the best organised and structured model of democratic political leadership so far. An important point is the strong link to ethical values and heritage which is emphasised by the RSS, which has a close link with the Government. Many BJP leaders were and are members of the RSS.

It is significant that two years since coming to power the Modi government, in striking contrast to the scandal a month UPA regimes I and II, it is free of any whiff of corruption. In addition, a lot of initiatives for development have been taken. The PM has taken a lead in improving the international image of our country.

In view of these, I am sure that we can look forward to good governance and a great future for us as citizens of India.

The wide-ranging cabinet reshuffle in July 2016 by Modi showed that meritocracy prevails in the Modi government. Performers have been rewarded and non-performers have been quietly dropped.

There is one additional major aspect that needs to be noticed. Modi as CM in Gujarat mentored two successors – Amit Shah and Saurabh Patel. As PM he has been mentoring a whole set of competent colleagues – Suresh Prabhu, Manohar Parrikar, Ravi Shankar Prasad and Nirmala Sitharaman. This ensues that the Modi effect in politics is not a temporary flash in the pan of Indian politics, but has a lasting legacy.

Modi government thus passes both our tests for democratic leadership. This is perhaps the best type of well-structured political leadership we have had in Independent India so far.

## Appendix 4

# Gujarat Model of Panchayati Raj: Downgrade for Democracy?

Mani Shankar Aiyar, the articulate Congreess MP in an op-ed article in *The Times of India* (Chennai), dated 30th June 2016 – 'A Downgrade for Democracy' – has said,

> "If, as *The Hindu*'s exclusive on Wednesday indicates, Prime Minister Narendra Modi was to close down the Ministry of Panchayati Raj, it would confirm one's worst fears about his government's hypocritical approach to grassroots democracy for grassroots development."

As an ex-bureaucrat of the Gujarat cadre of the IAS, I humbly disagree with the stand taken by the honourable MP who was a distinguished member of the IFS, before entering politics.

Panchayati Raj has been a great dream for many generations of India's leaders. Gandhiji visualized Rama Rajya in India where villages would ensure good governance, peace and prosperity.

In fact, the idea of democratic decentralization was articulated by the Balwant Rai Mehta Committee on behalf of the Indian National Congress in the late '50s and early '60s.

After Gujarat was formed on 1st May 1960, in 1963 the Panchayati Raj was introduced in Maharashtra and Gujarat, largely based on the Balwant Rai Mehta Committee report. As luck would have it, Balwant Rai himself became the second Chief Minister of Gujarat and died tragically in 1965 in an air crash in Kutch during the Indo-Pak conflict. Nevertheless over the years, the functioning of the Panchayati Raj and the operational compulsions and real politic at the field level led to the de facto decentralization of powers that were decentralised back at the State level.

After the '60s the hold of the Indian National Congress weakened at the national level. Regional parties appealing to the limited area of the State became more powerful politically.

This was perhaps an unexpected consequence of the reorganisation of the States on the basis of language in 1956. Even before 1956, thanks to the strong and sometimes violent agitation for forming a Vishal Andhra on the basis of Telugu culminating in the tragic death of Potti Sreeramulu who took a fast unto death for this demand. Andhra Pradesh was formed from the erstwhile presidencies of Madras and Bombay plus the native State of Mysore.

Ironically in 2014 we witnessed a further split of Andhra Pradesh itself into the two States of Telangana and Andhra Pradesh!

1967 was a watershed year leading to the emergence of the Samyukta Vidhayak Dal (SVD) largely dominated by regional parties. The championing of the Panchayati Raj by the Central Government perhaps reflects its anxiety to ensure that inspite of the political clout of the regional parties, it retains a direct hold at the village level.

This real politic can easily be camouflaged as the Central Government's concern for democratic decentralization and empowering of the people at the grass roots.

After all, what does 'empowering' mean?

Empowering has two aspects. One is purely the legal framework conferring legitimacy and authority for governance. The second aspect which is really important and what really matters at the field level is access to funds. The 73rd and 74th Amendments of the Constitution spearheaded by Rajiv Gandhi and enacted into law, by his low profile successor PV Narasimha Rao was popularised in the media by the vigorous efforts of Mani Shankar Aiyar as his articulate and visible aide, tried to cover both these aspects.

From a macro point of view the 73rd and 74th Amendments placed India in the same position as Gujarat and Maharashtra were in 1963 when they first tried to implement the concept of democratic decentralization and empowering the people at the grass roots level based on the Balwant Rai Mehta Committee report.

These two States therefore had, based on their experience, come to realize that for good governance the effective power especially for regional parties who geographically influenced the State, should be at the State level.

By the time the Rajiv Gandhi inspired Panchayati Raj was introduced, regional parties had tasted power and had also defined their territories of political clout at the State level. A country of India's size can only operate as a union of States and even though modern technology and the digital era may provide the reach and capacity for micro management, when it comes to good governance and satisfying regional aspirations, perhaps India has to practice co-operative federalism with the States as the participating units. Grass roots empowerment directly from the centre of the type visualized has its inherent weakness.

Perhaps the current efforts of the Modi government represents at the national level the restructuring of governance based on the pragmatic lessons of Gujarat and Maharashtra which have maintained their positions as well-governed States for a long time. The Gujarat-Maharashtra model provides a ready, time-tested template on which to build good governance for the future without creating further tensions and frustrations.

## Appendix 5

# Can Modi Dismount the Hindutva Tiger?

Sagarika Ghose in an op-ed article in *The Times of India* (Chennai), August 17th 2016, titled 'Gau Raksha Vs Bull Run', has observed that Modi has attacked cow vigilantes but can he dismount the Hindutva tiger?

Elaborating her point in the article she says –

> "In 1996 Indira Gandhi imperiously stared down a storming of Parliament by cow agitators. Togadia has again called Modi 'anti-Hindu' and VHP has announced it will stage a 1966 type rally in November. If Modi doesn't confront them as Indira did, it will mean Togadia is having the last laugh. Or maybe this is just shadow boxing: keep the Hindutva agenda boiling in the background while outwardly speaking the language of 'Sabka Saath, Sabka Vikas'. Riding a tiger is often easier than dismounting from it."

My view is that Modi can and will gracefully dismount the tiger.

Here are some of the many reasons why this will happen:

- As Chief Minister of Gujarat from 2002 to 2014, Modi has already demonstrated that although when he came to power he had to face the consequences of 2002

Gujarat riots, as a result of which he earned the title of 'Hindu Hriday Samrat', for more than a decade he firmly focused his efforts on ensuring good governance and communal peace in Gujarat. He came up with innovative initiatives like vibrant Gujarat. Surprisingly, there were no major communal riots of the type that took place in 2002.

- It is true that perhaps for the first time in Indian political history a Chief Minister has directly become the Prime Minister of the country much against the observations, projections and conventional wisdom of the talking heads in the electoral and print media. Does it mean that Modi lacks the basic political wisdom of tackling the problem of communalism at the national level?

India is not Gujarat writ large. And the very fact that we are a huge country of sub continental dimensions with a population of 1.25 billion with a multi-religious, multi-ethnic, multi-lingual background provides a much greater scope for Modi as a political strategist in framing his political strategies.

- Although compared to many of his predecessors he has been the most publicly visible and articulate leader, he has been extremely careful, shrewd and wise in making his political observations on sensitive issues. In fact this upsets his 'secular' critics in the electronic and print media to such an extent that they literally whip up a chorus about his deafening silence on issues related to the comments made by the fringe elements of Hindutva in the BJP. As I have pointed out in my earlier

> articles what Modi and Mohan Bhagwat, Sar Sanghachalak of RSS, are doing is to re-structure and reinvent the RSS as an organization rooted in the soul of Indian culture which is Sanatana Dharma.

Sagarika Ghose, in her article goes on to observe:

> "In 1966 Indira Gandhi imperiously stared down a storming of Parliament by the cow agitators."

I happened to be working at that time as under-secretary in the political division of the Ministry of Home Affairs in the South Block and an eye witness to the event!

I remember that the agitation was a very very limited event which did not have wide impact. Fifty years ago, in 1966 India did not have the type of 24 × 7 electronic media and more importantly, the ever present social media. Today in 2016 the technology of SCAM (Social, Cloud, Analytics and Mobile) has empowered practically every person with an access to a smart phone to start a political debate on a global scale on any issue. The media has become a great megaphone and multiplier of the noise level and creates a misleading impression about the actual impact of any event, at the grass roots level.

Apart from all these factors, it is necessary to bring in an element of commonsense about the nature of any political party in assessing the impact of the cow vigilantes. In the ultimate analysis every party has a core set of principles in which every member believes. There is a wide spectrum of vies in every party. There are always fringe elements, who may have extreme views on some issues. A mature party like the BJP knows how to check those elements from highjacking the party.

It is interesting that in the same article Sagarika also speculates as follows:

> "... or is this all shadow boxing: keep the Hindutva agenda boiling in the background, while outwardly speaking the language of 'Sabka Saath, Sabka Vikas'?"

In his 13 year track record as CM Gujarat and two years as PM, Modi has given sufficient proof to demonstrate that he is fully committed to the values enshrined in the Constitution of India. Only the congenitally blind critics of Modi refuse to see this!

# Appendix 6

# Re-Engineering of Hindu Consolidation: Modi-Bhagwat Style

As the Modi government marches into its third year in office, the process of re-engineering Hindu consolidation which provides the legitimacy and the electoral clout for the BJP seems to be proceeding smoothly. This is thanks to the insights and designs of the two key leaders – Narendra Modi and Mohan Bhagwat.

The first element in the re-engineering is the core ideology. In an earlier article (*Bureaucracy Today*), I had suggested that the new brand name for the BJP's ideology should be Sanatana Dharma. As the BJP gets welded into a robust nationalistic party for governance occupying the right of centre in the political spectrum, it is the basic elements of this ideology which provide the underlining linking thread for the narrative. Sanatana Dharma consists of the following values which have been articulated repeatedly in the sacred texts of our Hindu religion.

1. Respect for all forms of life. Every living body has one thing in common. This is the *jivatma* (or the soul), God is *paramatma* the creator. *Jivatma* cannot be destroyed by fire, water, wind or anything else.

This principle is unlike other faiths, which consider that non-humans have no soul.

2. Hence the special and unique emphasis is on non-violence – *Ahimsa Paramo Dharma*.
3. Looking upon the entire world as a single family (*vasudhaiva kutumbakam*), is a principle that follows naturally. Hence the all inclusive universal approach.
4. Open-mindedness and welcoming noble thoughts from every direction, *'Aano bhadra'* is articulated in the *Rigveda*.
5. The concept of Dharma which is the right conduct. The emphasis is on speaking the truth and having the right conduct.

Shanti mantras at the end of all traditional education emphasise: Satyam Vada, Dharmam Chara, Acharyadevo bhava, Matrudevo bhava, Pitrudevo bhava and Atithidevo bhava.

Even the greatest and noblest ideology by itself cannot be the basis for building a robust political party which can govern a subcontinent, a huge country like India. It must have significant sections of the population who have a common approach and share the same values.

In choosing Sanatana Dharma as the ideology Narendra Modi and Mohan Bhagwat seem to have succeeded in establishing a strong pragmatic and effective alliance with two major groups. These are led by modern-minded gurus who draw their inspiration and message from the Sanatana Dharma and also street smart each one to highlight one aspect of Sanatana Dharma which finds a ready echo in the hearts and minds of a very large number of people. These gurus are not only street smart but also very effective communicators.

Two of them are Baba Ramdev and Sri Sri Ravi Shankar.

Baba Ramdev focuses on Yoga and Ayurveda. Sri Sri Ravi Shankar's focus is on Sudarshana Kriya. Over the years these two gurus have been able to attract a very large number of followers not only in India but in many parts of the world. They find in the ideology of the BJP a very great resonance and in a physical sense contribute a very large core of the population to support the BJP.

There is yet another group which Narendra Modi especially has been able to focus on and attract in all the years that he has been working as a member of the RSS and in the nearly one and a half decades, as the Chief Minister of Gujarat. Pragmatism and idealism are uniquely combined in the DNA of Gujaratis, which have made them successful in business and collective social mobilisation all over the world from times immemorial.

The third group are the non-resident Indians (NRIs). Gujaratis constitute a very significant and large part of these NRIs who have a special love for their country and their own State and even villages.

The role of the expatriates has been widely recorded so far as the overseas Chinese are concerned. What Modi has done is to effectively demonstrate that non-resident Indians are no less than the overseas Chinese when it comes to contributing for the development of their own country.

In short the robustness of BJP as a nationalist political party with long-term staying power as a party of governance occupying the right of centre in the political spectrum is a new reality that has been decisively established after the elections of 2014. This in itself is a historic step in the evolution of India as a modern democracy which can also ensure good governance.

## Appendix 7

# Regionalism Triumphs Over Irredentism

Irredentism according to *The Concise Oxford Dictionary* is a term that originated in the context of the 19th century Italian politics. It was used to describe the demand for the restoration of the territories lost by it.

According to an article by Swapan Dasgupta in *The Times of India* (Chennai edition), 4th September 2016, in the Indian context, this term was liberally bandied about pejoratively to describe the RSS demand for Akhand Bharat. Dasgupta goes on to focus in the article on the decision taken by the Mamata Banerjee government in West Bengal to substitute, the name of the State with Bangla/Bengal/Bangal.

Dasgupta traces in his insightful article the emotional attachment of the Bengalis to their language and the shared memories of an united Bengal. He traces the significance of the first partition of Bengal in 1905 initiated by the Viceroy Lord Curzon and the tragic partition of Bengal for the second time when India became independent in 1947. He ends the article by saying "even as India and Bangladesh move towards a stable relationship, the delusions of the past have finally been junked. Irredentism has been issued a death certificate decades after its actual death."

It is interesting that when we look at our history the

interplay between irredentism and regionalism seems to have been an under appreciated recurring theme. At least three parallel cases come readily to my mind.

The first and perhaps the oldest, is the Dravidian movement in Tamil Nadu which can be traced back to 1910 with the formation of the Justice Party. This party consisting of well to do leaders of the south Indian community who were not Brahmins. They and their party were focused on ensuring that the dominance of the Brahmins in Tamil Nadu under the British government, thanks to their taking up early to English education and their command over the English language, should be challenged. They succeeded in their effort and as the freedom movement gathered momentum, in the first three decades of the twentieth century, captured political power under the reform legislations successively enacted by the British to encourage local self-government.

By a curious twist of history, it was again the Brahmins who dominated the Congress Party which led the freedom movement and the Justice Party found itself supporting the British government in the '20s and '30s. The advent of Gandhiji brought a dramatic change in widening the appeal of the Congress and making it an umbrella party for the freedom struggle.

In 1946 the Justice Party had lost its momentum and was reborn as the Dravida Kazhagam (DK) under the leadership of redoubtable Erode V Ramaswamy Naicker popularly known as Periyaar. Ironically, he was a close associate of Rajaji and an active leader of the Congress party, who had radical ideas on social reform. He was a Kannadiga hailing from Erode and visualized Dravida Nadu as inclusive of all the southern States of Tamil Nadu, Andhra Pradesh, Telangana, Karnataka and Kerala. One strong element behind the Dravida concept was the unique and historic position of Tamil as an ancient classical language and linguistically the mother of Kannada, Malayalam and Telugu. The Dravidian movement not only emphasized the separate identity of the southern States and moved for social reform, abolition of differences between castes and social equality. Most importantly, it did not accept the concept of a united India. In short, the behaviour of the Tamils in the Dravidian movement was similar to the irredentists in the Italian movement led by Garibaldi and Mazzini in the 19th century.

Unfortunately, the rest of the southern States like Andhra, Kerala and Karnataka did not buy this idea championed by the Dravida Kazhagam and its offspring the Dravida Munnetra Kazhagam (DMK).

In fact, they claimed their own languages to be also ancient classical languages. Soon after the Atal Bihari Vajpayee government conferred the status of classical language on Tamil, in the year 2000, all the three also ended up getting a similar status.! This has been upheld recently by the Madras High Court. In short, regionalism had triumphed over irredentism.

A further reiteration of this trend is what happened in 2013 when Telangana was separated from Andhra Pradesh. It must be recalled, that soon after independence in 1947, it was the strong demand for Vishal Andhra as a State based on the Telugu language and the enormous emotional movement resulting in the fast unto death of Potti Sreeramulu in 1952 that compelled Jawaharlal Nehru to concede to the demand

and form Vishal Andhra including the regions of Madras presidency in British India, Telangana and Rayalaseema. The formation of Andhra gave a further boost to the linguistic re-organization of States which took place in 1956.

A third example of the triumph of regionalism is in Maharashtra. The separation of Gujarat and Maharashtra in 1960 as a result of the Samyukta Maharashtra and the Maha Gujarat movements following the 1956 linguistic re-organization of States did not put an end to the growth of regionalism. The formation of Shiv Sena in 1966 based mainly on job opportunities for Mumbaikars showed that regionalism can flourish on the basis of not only language but on economic factors.

Maharashtra has a remarkable place in Indian history. The coming together of the Maharashtrians under the inspired leadership of Chhatrapati Shivaji, who in turn was inspired by the vision of Samartha Ramdas, was a golden period in our history. The Maharashtrian confederacy in the 17th and 18th century dominated practically the whole of the country providing challenges to the authority of the Mughal empire and the emerging colonial powers of the British, French and the Portuguese.

The Shiv Sena by appealing to the Marathi Manus is similar to the irredentists of the Italian movement. Nevertheless today the demand for Vidarbha which is raised from time to time shows that the dynamics of irredentism versus regionalism is not a closed chapter in our country.

As has happened in Tamil Nadu, Andhra Pradesh and now Bengal, will Maharashtra also see regionalism triumph?

# Index